# AMERICA'S MONEY

*The Story of Our Coins and Currency*

# AMERICA'S MONEY

## The Story of Our Coins and Currency

### J. EARL MASSEY

THOMAS Y. CROWELL COMPANY
*New York   Established 1834*

Designed by Judie Mills

Manufactured in the United States of America

L. C. Card 68-31772

1   2   3   4   5   6   7   8   9   10

# PREFACE

The author's particular interest in the history of American coins, and his desire to understand what they meant to the people who used them generations ago, developed largely after he joined the Westchester County (New York) Coin Club in the 1930's. As a member, and later as an officer of the group, he found that one who took time to dig into the history of a coin could, in a talk or paper delivered at the group meeting, make that coin or any numismatic item "come alive" with interesting, little-known facts.

He soon discovered a surprising lack of published material about coins or other forms of money suitable for the average reader. Generally speaking, the available books are written by specialists for special groups of readers, either for coin collectors and numismatic students or for students of economics. Those written by numismatic authorities for collectors quite often assume considerable background knowledge on the part of the reader, as do textbooks for the students of banking and economics on the college level. Such books written about coins do not usually relate them to the history of their own time or even to other contemporary forms of money. As a result, the average reader gets only part of the story of the subject he is interested in and perhaps not the most significant part.

This book is intended to give the reader a brief, comprehensive, and clearly understandable account of all the coins that have been used by the American people. Its aims are to point out the importance of metallic currency in relation to other forms of money used in the various periods of national existence. It is primarily about coins in circulation and their everyday use by the people rather than about banking and finance. It deals briefly with paper money, but mainly as it relates to the supply of coins. A few of the people who played key roles in the production of coins are mentioned briefly as are some of the major political and economic changes in American history in which currency played an important part. The focus of the book is the usefulness of the coins and the roles they have played in the changing social, economic, and political structure of the nation.

In research preparatory to writing this book, the author was greatly assisted by members of the staff of the American Numismatic Society in New York, to which he belongs, and where much of the research was done. He wishes particularly to acknowledge invaluable assistance given by Dr. Richard P. Breaden, former librarian and editor of numismatic literature at the society, now librarian at St. Joseph's Seminary, Dunwoodie, New York, who helped in editing the book. Other society staff members who assisted the writer were Geoffrey H. North, the present librarian; Francis D. Campbell, assistant librarian; Henry Grunthal, curator of European and modern coins; and Leslie A. Elam, editor of publications.

The writer particularly wants to acknowledge the assistance given by D. Wayne Johnson, founding editor of *Coin World,* who helped in editing the book, and by Robert I. Nesmith, a foremost authority on Spanish and Spanish-American coins, who furnished information concerning their use by our American ancestors. For data supplied by Miss Eva Adams, director of the U.S. Mint, and others in the U.S. Treasury Department, the author is also grateful.

Invaluable information has been obtained from numerous publications, including articles in *The Numismatist,* the publication of the American Numismatic Association, and *The Numismatic Scrapbook Magazine.*

J. EARL MASSEY

# CONTENTS

# 1

# TEMPORARY SOLUTIONS: GOODS INSTEAD OF MONEY

When money is mentioned in the United States today what is almost always meant are the coins and paper currency issued by the federal government. It may be vaguely recalled that in the past other materials, such as Indian wampum, have been used as money, and that sometimes people simply bartered —that is, exchanged—one kind of goods for another, without needing money at all. But now the use of coins and paper bills is so nearly universal in buying and selling that they are taken for granted. Why they have taken the place of all other types of money in this country and have almost completely replaced barter as well is seldom asked.

The reasons why coins and paper money are preferred will be seen very quickly after a glance back to the early days in North America before they were in common use. It should be kept in mind, though, that the advantages of using coins were not new to the American colonists. They and their ancestors in

England, Holland, and elsewhere in Europe had been using them for centuries. The only reason that they did not use coins for most business transactions in the colonies was that there were not enough of them to go around. The majority of people had very few coins and were therefore largely dependent upon bartering the produce of their farms.

This custom of bartering one commodity for another was, of necessity, widely accepted. There was so little metallic money available that the early colonists had not only to trade but even to pay their taxes with farm produce. They continued using money substitutes for a long time. Exchanges often took place in country stores, where nearly everything that the local countryside produced and everything that the people who lived in it might need could be found. A few such stores still exist in rural regions. A farmer may bring in a basket of eggs, a crate of poultry, or other products of his farm and receive in exchange a pound of cheese, a bag of sugar, articles of clothing, hardware, or some other necessity.

MONEY SUBSTITUTES

When we explore the nation's history in terms of coin and other money, the definition of money expands. For in reality money is any commodity of exchange. During our historical development it has taken many forms, meeting the varied needs of people in different places, times, and circumstances.

The colonial period 1607–1775 was a time of money complications as well as other hardships. Each colony, though it had much in common with its neighboring settlements, had its own particular products and peculiar problems of exchange. In that age of barter and commodity currency (which people then referred to as "country pay"), the list of forms money took was almost endless.

In the various colonies, government authorities specified the commodities that could be used as money in payment of public and private debts. They sometimes tried to set the exchange values of each product, though these values were not always observed. Since the values naturally depended upon supply and demand, they constantly changed.

SCARCITY OF COINS

From the beginnings of colonization there were limited numbers of coins in circulation. Some of these coins had been brought over by English and other European settlers. But the newcomers were usually from the poorer classes and had little money to bring along with them. Furthermore, coins brought to America by immigrants or by trade tended to flow back almost at once to Europe to purchase articles needed by the settlers in their conquest of the new land—agricultural tools and equipment for the home and business establishments.

Despite the general lack of coins, the prices of

articles bought and sold were reckoned in terms of coin denominations. In the English colonies, for example, values were expressed in *pounds, shillings,* and *pence* (pennies) ; in New Amsterdam, in terms of the Dutch *guilders, stivers,* and *florins.* In Delaware the Swedish settlers priced their products in their native *dalers* and *skillings,* while in the French settlements on the Gulf of Mexico people dealt in *livres, picaillions,* and *sous.*

ODD MONEY SUBSTITUTES

Powder and shot, much in demand in those days, were commonly used as money in the various colonies and at a later date in frontier settlements. In both Maryland and Virginia powder and shot were for a period almost the only media in which ship duties were paid. Among the early settlers of the Carolinas, rice, indigo, tar, pitch, and other products of the farms and forests served as currency in the absence of coins.

Nails, also used as money in the colonies, were scarce and costly until a nail-cutting and heading machine was invented late in the 1700's. Until then, the nails the blacksmith had to make by hand were valued in terms of pennies. The terms "tenpenny nail," "twentypenny nail," and the like remain today as reminders of the days when nails were money. Since nails were far from plentiful, most houses in the colonial period were built with wooden pegs, but nails were nevertheless often used, and abandoned houses were sometimes burned down for the nails that might be salvaged from them. To discourage this practice in Virginia, colonial authorities in 1646 offered to pay the owner of the house the cost of the nails if he would refrain from using the torch.

Indian corn, so called because it was a native New World product originally grown by the Indians, was very commonly used as money. Connecticut, for example, at an early date set the amount of corn that could be exchanged for labor, cattle, and other commodities.

## TOBACCO AS MONEY

Early in the history of Virginia and Maryland tobacco became the main crop and the principal form of money. Like corn, it was a native American product of Indian cultivation and was in great demand in England and Europe. John Rolfe, who married the Indian princess Pocahontas, is said to have started the commercial growing of tobacco in Virginia in 1612. In 1619, the first law passed by the first General Assembly at Jamestown made tobacco the official currency of the colony, fixing its price at 3 shillings a pound for the best grade and 18 pence a pound for the "second sorte," or lower grade. In that year a number of prospective brides were sent over from England. Lonesome settlers wanting to marry paid for their passage at the rate of 100 to 150 pounds of tobacco for each bride. As the most important single commodity currency in the southern seaboard colonies, tobacco became the mainstay of their early prosperity and gave them a highly favorable trade balance.

Like many other substitutes for money, tobacco presented special problems. It varied greatly in quality and could not be easily transported and preserved. The biggest problem, however, was overproduction. Although tobacco had been valued at 3 shillings a pound in 1619, by 1645 it was so abundant that it was worth only 1½ pence a pound. By 1665, despite various laws passed to restrict tobacco planting, the price had slumped to 1 penny a pound, a mere fraction of its original worth.

Realizing the inconvenience of a type of currency that was subject to uneven production and decreasing value, Virginia passed a law in 1633 requiring that "all contracts, bargains, pleas and judgements" be made in coin. Since few coins were in circulation, however, the law was ineffective.

Equally ineffective were laws restricting production of tobacco. Virginia, in an effort to raise the price of the product, ordered in 1640 the burning of all the bad and half of the good grades of leaf. In 1666 Maryland and Virginia ratified a treaty to stop the planting of tobacco for one year. These laws, and various others ordering other commodities to be used as money substitutes, caused only a temporary, ineffectual halt in tobacco production.

In 1683 the low price of the product caused many

Virginians to sign petitions requesting another year's cessation of tobacco planting. When the authorities refused this request, certain rebellious people went about destroying tobacco plants. These "tobacco riots" caused the authorities to pass a law declaring that persons in bands of eight or more who destroyed tobacco plants would be adjudged traitors and suffer death.

TOBACCO NOTES

Though tobacco persisted as a currency in Virginia, Maryland, and the Carolinas for some time thereafter, it was gradually replaced by a more convenient and more modern form of money—tobacco notes. These notes, legalized in Virginia in 1727, were one of the earliest forms of paper money. Each note represented a quantity of tobacco of a particular grade deposited in a regional warehouse. The notes were one of the most trustworthy and useful kinds of colonial money for many decades and had relatively wide circulation.

Similarly, warehouse receipts were used in the handling of rice and other commodities in the Carolinas. As in the case of tobacco, the warehouse was the "bank" in which the product was deposited and kept temporarily without undue risk and transportation expense, while the paper representing the deposit could be used as money anywhere in the colonies. This form of paper money was so widely acceptable that it was used in trade between different colonies as well as within the colony in which it was issued. It contributed greatly to the general prosperity.

During the period when tobacco was the principal currency in Virginia in all sorts of business and legal transactions, coins might, nevertheless, be required in exceptional cases. For example, a law of 1643 specified that horse breeders could demand metallic money for their animals. This law was intended to encourage the breeding of horses, then so important in farming and transportation.

WAMPUM

In New England, furs, grain, and fish were among the first items used for purposes of exchange, including the payment of private debts and taxes. Pork, beef, wool, corn, and livestock, as well as other commodities, were added later. One form of commodity exchange, wampum (figure 1), a type of Indian ornament, was early adopted as legal currency in Massachusetts. In 1637, according to Massachusetts records, "it was ordered that wampumeage [sometimes wampum was known as peage] should pass at six a penny for any sum under 12 pence."

Like tobacco and other commodity money, wampum varied in quality and value. It consisted of the inner whorls of seashells. These were polished, made into beads, and strung together in belts or sashes. Generally the color of the beads was either black or white, the black being rarer and about double the

*Figure 1. Wampum of the type used in seventeenth-century Massachusetts.* (Museum of the American Indian, Heye Foundation)

value of white. Since white beads could be dyed black, wampum was often counterfeited, causing changes in its value from time to time and from colony to colony. In Connecticut in 1648 four white beads had the value of a penny, while in Massachusetts the exchange rate was usually from six to eight beads for a penny.

Wampum was widely used in New England, probably more so than in any other part of the colonies. It was a convenient currency in the beaver-skin trade with the Indians. Gradually, however, its disadvantages as a medium of exchange among the colonists began to be felt. Because of its relatively low unit value, a great deal of wampum was needed to exchange for more expensive goods. Imagine the amount of wampum necessary to buy an acre of land or a horse! The need for a more flexible currency caused Massachusetts to become in 1652 the first colony to mint coins of its own. Because of New England's extensive shipping trade, which was larger than that of the rest of the colonies, additional coins from other countries were brought in by New England vessels and were used extensively.

In New Netherlands wampum was the first legal currency, though it was subordinate to the silver coinage of the mother country, Holland. The Dutch settlers imported their wampum from the eastern end of Long Island, an important center of production. The price of wampum was fixed at six white beads for a stiver, but later dropped to eight. During the colonial period the Dutch were strong competitors of the English and are said to have provided possibly more coins for their settlers in New Amsterdam than did England in its colonies.

Beaver skins, which the Dutch colonists secured by trading wampum and other articles with the Indians, also became an important currency in New Netherlands. It was first rated at 8 florins or 160 stivers per skin, but later reduced to 6 florins. The wide acceptance of beaver skins among currency items was based on Europe's strong demand for them. The price of beaver in the colonies was rated by the pound as well as by the skin. In Massachusetts, it was receivable for debts at 10 shillings per pound.

Wampum and beaver skins were not the only media of exchange used in New England. The General Court of Massachusetts set the price for payments in various types of produce. In 1631 it ordered that corn should pass for payment of debts at the current selling price, unless coin or beaver skins were specified. As other crops of importance were introduced, they were generally added to the list of commodity money in Massachusetts. In 1640, when the price of corn was rated at 4 shillings per bushel, wheat and peas were marked at 6 shillings and rye and barley at 5 shillings.

The use of country produce such as grain for money naturally involved transportation costs. Colonial authorities, accepting produce for taxes, estimated their collection and haulage costs at about 10 per cent of the selling price of the commodity.

PROBLEMS WITH PERISHABLES
An example of the hazards of such transportation is provided by the records of a collection of 150 bushels

of peas for taxes one year in Springfield, Massachusetts. The local constable found that he could transport the public revenue most cheaply by boat on the Connecticut River. But when the craft passed over a falls, it shipped water and the peas were spoiled.

Colonial records leave little doubt as to the inconveniences and hazards of commodity money. Though coins were scarce, some merchants insisted on receiving them for their wares. Consequently, according to Governor of Massachusetts John Winthrop's *Journal* of October 1640, "men could not pay their debts though they had enough," and the prices commanded by land and cattle soon fell to one-half or even as little as one-fourth of their former valuation.

In colonial times it was customary to pay wages for hired servants and tradesmen with coins. When this was not possible, commodities of one kind or another had to suffice. When a servant had served his term of employment, quite often his master could not afford to rehire him, except on unreasonable terms. The case of a man named Rowley and his servant is cited in Winthrop's *Journal*. The master, forced to sell a pair of oxen to pay his servant wages, told him he could not keep him any longer, not knowing how to pay him next year. The servant answered that he would accept cattle as payment. "But how shall I [pay you] when all of my cattle are gone?" asked Rowley. The servant replied: "You shall then serve me, and so you may have your cattle again."

COINS FROM THE WEST INDIES

After 1650, as the colonies developed, trade began to play an increasingly important role in bringing additional coins into circulation. Continued demand for tobacco had early secured for the southern colonies a favorable balance of trade. The Middle Atlantic colonies grew grain to be shipped abroad. New England merchants played a leading role in international as well as intercolonial trade. Their vessels took cargoes of dried fish and lumber to the West Indies, where sugar and molasses were obtained; rum made in New England from the molasses was then shipped to Africa, which provided slaves for sale in the West Indies. Known as the "triangular trade," this commerce enabled New England vessels to bring to the colonies a large assortment of the coins of many nations, especially Spanish silver and gold pieces.

New England shipmasters soon developed a worldwide trade, carrying West Indian tobacco and sugar to Europe and bringing back from overseas ports many of the products in demand on the mainland and in the island colonies. These ships of sail were to form the basis of the nation's future sea power.

As a result of such trade, there was a marked increase in the supply of badly needed coins. These coins, chiefly silver and gold, were of Spanish, English, Dutch, and French origin. A large number of them came from the West Indies, which were peopled largely by these four nationalities and which had a brisk trade with the mainland colonies and with Europe. Ships from New England and New York were active in supplying provisions from the various seaboard colonies to the islands.

Most of the coins coming from the West Indies were Spanish, minted in Spain, Peru, and above all in Mexico, which had especially rich silver mines. For many generations, Spanish coins were to constitute the main supply of "hard" money used in America. Unfortunately, as fast as the metallic money flowed into the colonies, it flowed out to Europe and elsewhere to secure the wares and necessities not yet being made by the colonists themselves. This left only a part of the money supply in circulation.

DWINDLING COMMODITY MONEY

There was less official sanction and less general use of commodity money in the eighteenth century than in the seventeenth. By 1700 most of the statutes making tobacco, pelts, powder, shot, cattle, and grain "legal tender" had been repealed. This meant that these forms of money were no longer acceptable in payment of taxes or other debts, except in the frontier settlements where the shortage of coins was still acute. In eastern Tennessee and Kentucky deerskins and raccoon pelts were receivable for taxes and served other currency needs as late as the early 1800's.

Some of the later uses of commodity currency are noteworthy. In Iowa in 1840, for instance, it was reported that the marriage fee was three goatskins or four bushels of potatoes. Later still, in the more remote regions of Oregon, it is said that the only money at one time consisted of livestock. For example, a hog was valued at $1, a sheep at 50 cents. Turkeys were worth 25 cents each, and a dog 12½ cents. Thus, if Mr. Jones owed Mr. Smith $4 and 9 pence (pence were an English denomination then used locally in reckoning money), he might pay him with five hogs and receive in change one sheep, one turkey, and a pup.

In money-scarce California during the 1849 gold rush, a pinch of gold dust served to buy a prospector a drink. And, of course, the country store has continued the tradition of commodity exchange down to the present century. But for the most part the colonists in the more populated areas realized that commodity money presented too many problems to be a workable method of exchange. They turned to coins and currency as a more acceptable solution. But these also presented problems which had to be dealt with.

# 2

# EARLY COINS AND
# CURRENCY PROBLEMS

The colonial period was one of intense rivalries
among the colonizing powers. England, Holland,
and France competed for footholds in the New
World, where Spain had long been dominant because of its early discoveries and conquests. Although
England had defeated the Spanish Armada in 1588,
it was not able to secure a permanent settlement on
the North American continent until Jamestown,
Virginia, was established in 1607. England's serious
competitors were successively Spain, Holland, and
France. Spain, once powerful, was a diminishing
power during the period of British colonization of
America. Holland, an ascending rival, had to yield
eventually to England's greater strength, ceding New
Amsterdam in 1664. England's rivalry with France
culminated in the French and Indian War of the
mid-1700's, when the English colonists fought beside
the mother country to drive France from the continent. Later, during the American Revolution,

*16*

France allied itself with the former English colonists against England and was instrumental in helping them to gain independence.

MERCANTILISM AND THE SCARCITY OF COINS

The number of coins the colonists could acquire through foreign trade was largely determined by the policies of the colonizing powers. These countries believed in an economic system known as "mercantilism." This system was based partly on the idea that a nation's wealth depended on its supply of precious metals, specifically gold and silver. Therefore, they adopted policies that would enable them to acquire large amounts of coin, often at the expense of their colonies. For example, the mother country would try to sell to its colonies more than it bought from them, and the colonists would be forced to pay out most of their coins in making up the difference. As a result, English settlers in the New World were often drained of the little hard money they had.

Even if England had wanted to provide its colonists with enough coins for their needs, it would not have been able to. England had scarcely enough for its own use at home. In fact, the colonies proved an important source of coins for the mother country. As they developed and gathered in coins, mostly through other sources of trade, they bought goods from England with hard currency. Thus the flow of coin was constantly toward England. It is estimated that the average coin remained in circulation in the colonies only for a period of several months. Commodities shipped to England, instead of bringing back coins, were more often used to pay debts owed there or to purchase goods needed in America.

One of the biggest single shipments of coins from England during the colonial period was £187,000, chiefly in Spanish dollars, sent to Massachusetts in 1749. The shipment, from a grateful mother country, was in repayment of military expenses incurred by the colony in leading the 1745 expedition which captured the French fortress of Louisbourg on Cape Breton Island. It served as a considerable boost to the Massachusetts economy.

England's payment to one of its own colonies in foreign rather than in British money reflected the shortage of coins. The mother country had long used Spanish and other European currencies, particularly in shipments of money abroad. For centuries before the American colonies were established and all during the colonial period, England found it necessary from time to time to forbid the export of British coins in trade transactions with other nations and with its colonies in order to keep gold and silver pieces at home. As early as 1200, "exchanges" had been established to prevent or control the outflow of native currency and to convert it into foreign currency for payments abroad. In fact, during the colonial period paper "bills of exchange" frequently took the place of metallic money in domestic and foreign trade transactions.

England's measures to prevent the shipment of coins overseas were often directed against speculators who bought and sold precious metals. Such speculators found ways of avoiding restrictions. They profited by shipping the metals, including British coin, to other countries where their values were at times higher than in England.

In spite of so many restrictions, some British coins got to America and began to circulate. Among the pieces used in the colonies (figure 2) were the gold *guinea* and the silver *shilling* and *sixpence*. The guinea got its name from the fact that the gold it contained came from the Guinea coast of Africa. It was worth 21 shillings, whereas the pound (a monetary unit rather than a coin) consisted of 20 shillings, each worth 12 pence (pennies). The gold *sovereign* is an English coin valued at a pound. Records reveal very little circulation in America of other English coins, such as the *crown* (worth 5 shillings), the *half crown,* and the copper *halfpenny* and *farthing* pieces. The British copper penny was not minted until 1797. (These copper pieces are not to be confused with the colonial copper token pieces issued in England and America, often without official approval.)

The southern colonies had a favorable trade balance with the mother country, largely because of their tobacco exports. Therefore a larger percentage of British coins circulating in the colonies were to be found in the South than in the North. On the other hand, since New England and the Middle

*Figure 2. (a) English halfpenny, 1772. (b) Crown, circa 1640. (c) Queen Anne shilling. (d) Five-guinea piece, 1709. (American Numismatic Society)*

Atlantic colonies engaged in a sizable trade with Spain, Holland, France, and their colonies, the coins of those countries circulated more widely in New England and the Middle Atlantic colonies than in the South. Of course, through trade among the colonies coins flowed from one to another.

PIRATES AND BUCCANEERS AS A SOURCE OF COINS

Many coins were brought into the American colonies by pirates or buccaneers. Pirates were sea robbers who lived by plundering ships or even coastal towns. Buccaneers were originally quite different. They were mainly English or French sailors, many of whom lived on the Spanish West Indian island of Santo Domingo. They used to kill the wild cattle and pigs that ran loose there and smoke the meat on a grill called the *boucan,* which gave them their name of buccaneers. Because Spain refused to recognize the right of other nations to participate in trade or settlement in the West Indies, the buccaneers resorted to smuggling and other illegal practices in order to sell their cured meat. In course of time they became little better than pirates. Initially, however, they had the sympathy of their home governments, which resented Spain's vast monopoly in the New World.

Both pirates and buccaneers were active in the waters of the Spanish Main (the southern Caribbean Sea) during the last half of the seventeenth and the first half of the eighteenth centuries. They proved a source of gold and silver both in coin and in other forms. New England ports offered them open haven, where they could spend the booty that had been taken from Spanish treasure ships. Eventually, however, the buccaneers lost all the glamour of their early status and were considered no better than pirates. Both pirating and buccaneering were largely stamped out during the first half of the eighteenth century.

FRENCH COINS

Among the early coins that circulated in the French colonies, and to some extent in the English, were those of French origin (figure 3) . These included the *écu, livre, sol* (worth $\frac{1}{20}$ livre), *sou,* and the gold *Louis d'or.* During the seventeenth and eighteenth centuries, the écu was a large dollar-size coin valued at 3 livres. The silver livre, which was replaced by the *franc* in 1795, was worth 20 sous (halfpennies) . The Louis d'or, so-called for having been first struck by Louis XIII in 1640, was commonly called a *pistole* or French guinea. Its value ranged from about $3.84 to $5.79. After 1795 it was replaced by the gold *Napoleon,* valued at 20 francs ($3.86) and named after the French emperor who took power after the French Revolution and changed the nation's coinage system. The name of the old French coin called the *picayune* or *picaillion* was often applied in the southern colonies to the Spanish *medio* or *half-real,* which was $\frac{1}{16}$ of the Spanish dollar, and later to the U.S.

*Figure 3. (a) Louis d'or, representing Louis XIV, 1662. (b) Double sol, Louis XV, 1743.* (American Numismatic Society)

half-dime and 5-cent pieces. Even today something of small value is often referred to as "not worth a picayune."

### SPANISH, PORTUGUESE, AND DUTCH COINS

Spanish coins (figure 4) were so important in colonial America that the next chapter will be devoted to them. Of the pieces most commonly used in trade and commerce, the greatest in value was the *eight-real* piece (piece of eight), better known as the Spanish dollar and worth about the same as the U.S. dollar. It was divided into the *four-real* or half dollar; the *two-real,* equivalent to the U.S. quarter; the *real,* worth 12½ cents; and the *medio* or *half-real,*

worth 6¼ cents. All were silver, as was the "base pistareen." Valued at about ⅕ of a dollar, this was a debased two-real piece, coined at the home mints in Spain, whereas the bulk of Spanish coins came from the nation's colonial mints. Spanish gold coins included the *doubloon,* originally worth about $16 but later reduced in value, and the *pistole,* worth about ¼ of a doubloon.

Portuguese gold coins circulating in the American colonies included the *moidore* and the *johannes* or "joe," named for John V of Portugal (figure 4). Both were made of gold mined in Brazil. The moidore was at one time worth about $3.27; the joe about $8.81. There were, in addition, *half-joes* and *cruzadoes,* some struck in gold, others in silver, which had various values.

Colonial records show the use of the Dutch *rix-dollars* and *guilders,* of various values; *ducatoons* or silver-dollar-size coins of the Low Countries of Europe; and gold *sequins* of Venice or Turkey, worth about $2.25.

VARYING VALUES OF COINS

During the colonial period the values placed on coins other than those of the mother country varied

*Figure 4. (a) Spanish four-real piece, Philip IV, 1664. (b) Two-real, 1774. (c) Real, 1757. (d) Doubloon, 1683. (e) Portuguese "half-joe," 1773.* (American Numismatic Society)

from time to time and from colony to colony in much the same way as the prices of commodities. Early attempts to value coins uniformly in the colonies failed, since each colony had a separate government motivated by interests of its own. No central authority, not even the British Crown, was able to achieve monetary uniformity, though the Crown often issued proclamations for the regulation of coin values.

As with commodities, coin values were expressed in terms of the English denominations of pounds, shillings, and pence, even when no British coins were in any way concerned. The price of the Spanish dollar varied greatly in the colonies. For example, it was worth 5 shillings in Georgia and 8 shillings in New York. The actual worth of the Spanish dollar in silver content was relatively stable at 4 shillings and 6 pence, but colonies that needed to attract hard money—that is, coins—would very often overvalue the coin and its subdivisions. Naturally the coins would be most used in those colonies where they could buy more for their face value. Thus, the coins traveled back and forth periodically among the colonies, always available in the greatest number where they could fetch the highest price.

In 1704 and 1707 proclamations were issued by England forbidding a higher rating than 6 shillings for the Spanish dollar. Like so many such orders, this one seems to have been largely ignored in business transactions. Earlier, in 1679, the British governor of Virginia had found a way of profiting from the fluctuating currency. He had accumulated a considerable supply of Spanish coin when the dollar was valued at 5 shillings. He then arbitrarily declared its value to be 6 shillings and paid his troops in the money he had thus depreciated. But since his own salary and the taxes he collected were reckoned in the same terms, his gain may have been less than he calculated.

CLIPPING OF COINS

Many of the coins in circulation were clipped by unscrupulous persons who scraped some of the metal from the edges to steal silver. In doing so they reduced the metal content, which determined the intrinsic value of the pieces. This practice flourished toward the close of the seventeenth century and persisted even later despite efforts of the authorities to curb it. Many Spanish and other early coins, called "cobs," were of irregular shapes because they were cut from crude silver bars and struck from rough dies. For this reason clipping was not always readily recognized. Only by weighing the coins could their true value be determined. This was actually done by merchants and others dealing with quantities of money during the colonial period and as long thereafter as clipped and badly worn coins remained in circulation. Small scales for weighing such coins became standard equipment in business establishments and were usually placed alongside the list of current local values of the numerous kinds of foreign coins in circulation. One of the main reasons for coin scales was that coins shipped to England were acceptable only by weight. The colonial business-man ordering goods from England could not stay in business very long without weighing his coins.

Most colonists, who could never seem to get enough coins for their daily transactions, were less particular. Clipped coins continued to circulate freely among them, while whole ones were hoarded by businesses requiring full-weight coins. How in-ferior coins drive good coins out of circulation in this way was explained by Sir Thomas Gresham in 1559 to Queen Elizabeth and is known as Gresham's Law. This "law" has operated many times with coins used in the United States, even after the nation was founded and had its own mint.

It may seem surprising that such confusing condi-tions of exchange did not completely stifle trade among the colonies. Whenever, for example, a New Yorker tried to do business with a Philadelphian, their contract had to state whether the pay was to be in "New York currency" or "Philadelphia currency." Then the number of Spanish dollars, or other coins, that passed between them had to be adjusted ac-cording to the value they held at that moment in the colony agreed upon. As foreign trade increased, the situation became almost hopelessly complicated, and the difficulty was increased by the variety of foreign coins in use and the different valuations given them in different areas. Each colony set prices on both coins and commodities every year. But these were not always the prices they actually brought in the market.

Take the case of Madam Knight, a Boston school-mistress, who journeyed through New Haven, Connecticut, in 1704 and wrote (in *The Journals of Madam Knight,* 1825, edited by Theodore Dwight) as follows:

> *They give the title of merchant to every trader who rates their goods according to the time and specie [kind of money] they pay in:* viz., *Pay, Money. Pay as money, and trusting.* Pay *is grain, pork, beef, etc., at the prices set by the General Court that year.* Money *is pieces of eight, reals, or Boston or Bay shillings (as they call them), or good hard money, as sometimes silver coin is termed by them. Also, wampum— Indian beads which serve for change.* Pay as money *is provisions, as aforesaid, [but] one third cheaper than as the Assembly or General Court sets it; and* Trust, *as they and the merchant agree for time.*
>
> *Now, when the buyer comes to ask for a commodity, sometimes before the merchant answers that he has it, he says, "Is your pay ready?" Perhaps the chap replies "Yes." "What do you pay in?" says the merchant. The buyer having answered, then the price*

*is set. Suppose he wants a sixpenny knife,*
*in pay it is 12d—in pay as money eight*
*pence, and hard money its own price, viz.,*
*6d. It seems a very intricate way of trade*
*and what Lex Mercatoria had never*
*thought of.*

The Boston or Bay shillings Madam Knight
referred to were the shillings coined in Massachusetts in 1652. Her mention of wampum indicates
that Indian money was being used among the colonists themselves for small change. "Lex Mercatoria"
refers to an English law regulating merchants'
transactions.

SMALL-CHANGE PROBLEMS

Throughout the colonial period, the colonists were
handicapped by a shortage of coins of small denominations. There was no small copper coin in
circulation, such as the English penny or the U.S.
1-cent piece. About the smallest piece available was
the Spanish medio or half-real (worth $6\frac{1}{4}$ cents).
Occasionally there was an English sixpence, a silver
piece (worth about 12 cents). Most widely circulated of all the small coins was the Spanish real
($12\frac{1}{2}$ cents). For smaller change, Indian wampum
and other substitutes had to be used.

Many writers dealing with the colonial period
point out that change was sometimes created by
cutting up the Spanish dollar into small pieces, including eighths and sixteenths. But James Risk

wrote in the journal *Numismatic Review* (Vol. 2, No. 2, 1961) that this was not done in the continental American colonies. This idea grew, he believes, out of some very small, irregularly shaped Spanish coins such as those struck in Guatemala during colonial times, which might be mistaken for "cut" coins. "The myth was given life," he says, "by the later practise of cutting dollars to provide minor coins that was adopted by the governments of British West Indian Islands at the very end of the 18th century and at the beginning of the 19th."

COLONIAL COINS

In view of the scarcity of coins, especially those of small denominations, and the confusion of coin values from colony to colony, two questions naturally come to mind. Why did not the colonies make their own coins? And why did they not work together in solving their money problems? The answer to the first question is that they did coin money—but not often and not enough. Although the colonies lacked funds and mineral resources, they did occasionally make separate efforts to produce their own coins, but the numbers were small and could not fill the needs of all the colonies. Besides, in order to issue coins the colonies nearly always had to go against the policies of the mother country and even break its laws.

The answer to the second question is that the colonies did try, once in awhile, to cooperate in giving a uniform value to money. But they did not try hard enough to overcome the many obstacles. The truth is that until they at last united to defy England in the American Revolution, the colonies did not have a very good record of working together. Not until they had been a single nation for nearly a decade did they reach agreement on a uniform coinage. During colonial times there was only one readily available coinage upon which the colonists could rely. That was the Spanish dollar and its parts. Though often badly worn, clipped, and abused, these silver pieces still represented the best available standard of money and the best means of measuring values. They were therefore continuously used.

# 3

# THE SPANISH DOLLAR

"Pieces of eight, pieces of eight," screamed the old pirate's parrot aboard the *Hispaniola* in Robert Louis Stevenson's classic, *Treasure Island*. When we read about pieces of eight (also known as Spanish dollars) in works of fiction and history, they seem romantic and far removed from everyday life. But to the early colonists, these coins were as real and familiar as any U.S. coin is to Americans today. In colonial financial accounts the Spanish dollar was listed as a piece of eight or as a *piastre*. To the Spanish it was the eight-real piece (figure 5a), later called a *peso*. More often the coin used for small purchases was some fraction of the piece of eight: the four-real, the two-real or double-real, the real, or the medio or half-real (figure 5b).

Today the U.S. half dollar is sometimes referred to as "four bits" and the quarter as "two bits." These terms, among the oldest in the American monetary vocabulary, had their origin in the col-

*33*

*Figure 5.* (a) *Spanish eight-real piece, circa 1580; often called a "piece of eight."* (b) *Half-real piece, 1823.* (American Numismatic Society)

onists' use of Spanish coins. In colonial times the Spanish real was generally referred to as a "bit" in the Southwest and West, a "ninepence" in New England and Virginia, a "shilling" in New York, and a "levy" (an abbreviation for 11 pence) in Pennsylvania. These terms show once again the widely different values placed on all coins by the various colonies.

Spanish coins came into the colonies from countless sources. They were brought mainly by American ships as a result of the West Indian and "triangular" trade and to a lesser extent by pirates and buccaneers from the Caribbean and by various European ships.

SPANISH COINS AS LEGAL TENDER IN AMERICA

Because there were very few English or domestic coins in colonial America, and because French and Dutch coins were also limited in supply, the colonists welcomed Spanish coins. No other country had mineral resources and production machinery equal to Spain's, particularly in its New World possessions of Mexico and Peru. Therefore, the supply of Spanish coins was greater than that of any other nation. The quality of these coins also caused them to be universally sought. Though the Spanish dollar varied in silver content from mint to mint and from time to time, it usually contained a large amount of the valuable metal. It was acceptable in all parts of the world, particularly in nations that did not have enough coins of their own. It provided, therefore, a kind of universal standard of value. Tradesmen in India, for instance, hoarded the Spanish dollar at one time in preference to other available coins. And in China, up to about a century ago, it was still the favorite piece of money.

By 1650—only a few decades after the first English settlements were established on the North American continent—the colonies of Virginia, Massachusetts, and Connecticut had passed laws making Spanish coin legal tender for all purposes. Virginia passed a law in 1645 making the Spanish dollar worth 6 shillings. Gradually all the colonies came to regard Spanish coins as legal tender, each colony, however, giving them a different legal valuation.

Generally they were overvalued—that is, given a value higher than the worth of the actual silver they contained.

The *real* (the word meant "royal money"), eight of which constituted a Spanish dollar, was a much older denomination than the dollar itself. It is said to have been coined as early as 1370, when Pedro the Cruel was king of Spain. In 1497 Ferdinand and Isabella decreed it the Spanish monetary unit. It was also during their reign that the first pieces of eight were struck in Spain. But by far the greatest number of pieces of eight and reals came from the mints that Spain established in its colony of Mexico.

THE FIRST NEW WORLD MINTS

In 1536, 256 years before the U.S. Mint was established in Philadelphia and 71 years before the English landed at Jamestown, the first mint in the New World was built in Mexico City. Spain had reaped vast riches in the capture and destruction of the principal Aztec city, upon the ashes of which the Mexican capital was built. Coins were first minted there in the names of Charles I and Joanna, who then ruled Spain.

Mexico was the main source of coins for the early Americans. Some idea of its importance as a supplier may be gained from an 1889 report issued by a Mexican mint. The report states that from 1537 to 1821 (when Mexico gained independence from Spain) more than two billion dollars' worth of silver coins had been struck. By 1889 the mammoth output, coming from eleven different mints over a period of 352 years, had climbed to $3,193,215,137.

Dollar-size pieces of eight were first struck in the Spanish colonial mints of Mexico and Peru in 1572 during the reign of Philip II. The fabulously rich silver deposits of both Mexico and Peru made possible a steady flow of coins for worldwide use from a number of mints in these countries.

Many of the early Spanish dollars and smaller pieces were "cobs," that is, formless slabs of silver stamped with designs which made them coins (figure 5a). On one side appeared a cross resembling a windmill and on the other the royal Spanish coat of arms. Later, rounded and milled coins with corrugated edges replaced these crude pieces. In Mexico in 1732, pieces with milled or corrugated edges were first issued. This was an important development in Spanish colonial coin production because it not only made the coins more attractive, but also made more difficult the practice of chipping or clipping away metal from a coin, since clipping visibly changed the milling. Nicely rounded coins of improved design, however, did not entirely replace the old worn and clipped pieces, and merchants still had to resort to scales for determining coin values.

Coins struck in Spain bore the legend HISPANIARUM REX (King of the Spains), while those minted at the colonial mints were marked HISPANIARUM ET IND REX (King of the Spains and the Indies). The famous pillar-type coins so familiar to the American colonists were minted only in the New World. These coins had two identical pillars imprinted on one side, representing the Pillars of Hercules (the two promontories on opposite sides of the Strait of Gibraltar), which were symbolic of Spanish power in those days (figure 4a).

ORIGIN OF THE WORD "DOLLAR"

It is interesting to note how the term "dollar" came to be applied to the Spanish coin. "Dollar" comes from the German word *thaler,* derived from *thal* (meaning "valley"). The thaler was a large silver coin struck late in the fifteenth century, about the same size as the Spanish piece of eight. A large number of these German coins were struck by the Count of Schlick in the little town of Joachimsthal in Bohemia and were first known as "Joachimsthalers," later abbreviated to "thalers." The English called the thaler a "dollar" and also applied the name to the Spanish coin of similar size and worth.

INFLUENCE ON U.S. COINAGE

When the United States adopted its own coinage system many years later it chose to use a decimal system rather than the shilling-pence system of the mother country, England. So influential was the Spanish dollar in the lives of Americans that they designed their own silver dollar to compare with it in size and value. Moreover, they matched the half dollar to the Spanish four-real coin and the quarter to the double-real.

The use of Spanish coins as the principal metallic money in colonial America undoubtedly accounts for the fact that the U.S. silver dollar closely resembled the Spanish dollar in size and silver content. This resemblance was a factor in making the new U.S. coins acceptable. In the early years of the mint's operation, however, production of coins was inadequate because of limited mint facilities, shortage of metal, and shortcomings in coinage laws. What is more, a large number of coins produced during the first thirty years of the mint's operation never got into circulation. They fell into the hands of metal speculators, who could melt them down or ship them out of the country at a profit. Thus, there was little choice but to continue using Spanish and other foreign coins.

The variety and amount of coin production in America greatly increased in the 1830's. By the early 1850's the nation had, for the first time, an adequate supply of its own coins in circulation. New mint machinery, big gold discoveries in California, and changes in the coinage laws all contributed to the increase in supply. Also, steps were taken to get badly worn and clipped Spanish pieces out of circulation. The minting of American small coins —the 3-cent silver piece beginning in 1851 and the copper 1-cent "flying eagle" in 1857 (figure 6) —helped to replace foreign coins. But the final

*Figure 6. (a) Three-cent silver, 1857. (b) One-cent "flying eagle," 1857.* (American Numismatic Society)

blow to the Spanish dollar was a law passed in 1857 declaring that foreign coins could no longer be used as legal tender. Even at that late date, however, some three million dollars' worth of the Spanish coins were still being used. Many of these circulated in the less settled regions of the country, where some of the fractional pieces were still to be found years later. Thus, Spanish coins were used in America until enough U.S. coins were available to take their place. It was only gradually and reluctantly that the curtain fell on the era of the Spanish dollar. Long cherished as the world's most famous coin, it is now almost forgotten.

# 4

# AMERICAN COINS
# FOR AMERICANS

To have coins of their own was an important goal of the American colonists, who struggled with crude methods of bartering and used a variety of foreign coins. They were repeatedly prevented from reaching this goal by having insufficient resources and, more seriously, by the laws and attitudes of the British authorities.

PRIVATE COINERS

A number of coins or tokens were made specifically for the colonial Americans and a few were made by them. In most cases they were minted in England by private coiners or promoters for their own profit and not with the intention of providing sound money. Although several of the colonial issues were authorized by the British government, these too were often promoted with an eye to profit.

During the entire colonial period—the 150 or more years between the early settlements and the Revolutionary period—the only important American-made coins were those minted by the Massachusetts Bay Colony beginning in 1652. The colony's minting activities lasted for about thirty years and were finally suppressed as illegal by the English. Less important were the copper tokens privately made by John Higley in Granby, Connecticut, between 1737 and 1739.

COPPER PIECES PREDOMINATE

All of the colonial pieces made in England and America were of small denominations. Some were made of silver, but most were of copper or baser metal mixtures. They helped to satisfy the colonists' need for small change, though the colonists resented the fact that many of their coins had less pure metal in them than the coins minted by the English government. Most of the colonial issues were small ones of limited and local scope. They supplemented the general supply of coins only momentarily. But to students of American history and collectors they are of interest far beyond their original value.

Although the Bermudas, off the eastern coast of the United States, are now a British colony, in the early days of English colonization in America they were claimed as part of Virginia. They were named the Somers Islands after Sir George Somers, who was shipwrecked there in 1609 while transporting settlers to the two-year-old colony of Virginia. The setting of Shakespeare's play *The Tempest* is believed to have been suggested by the incident. The islands had been discovered more than a century earlier by a Spaniard, Juan de Bermúdez, and were known to the Spanish as the Bermudas—the name later adopted by the English. Shakespeare calls them "the much-vexed Bermoothes."

On his way to the West Indies, Bermúdez left behind a few pigs. By the time Somers arrived, their descendants were running wild on the island in great numbers. Recalling this fact, the figure of a hog was portrayed on the face of the Somers Islands coins, the first issue of money for an English American colony. Consequently, the pieces, which were made of brass or a similar metal mixture in about 1616, are sometimes referred to as "Hogge Money" or "Hoggies." They were presumably issued in England, though little is known of their origin. They are of twopenny, sixpenny, and shilling denominations and have on one side the imprint of a full-rigged ship with the flag of St. George on each of its four masts. These coins are quite rare today.

MASSACHUSETTS COINAGE

Good fortune, it seemed, smiled upon the sturdy folk of the Massachusetts Bay Colony when they made the first coins in America in 1652. The mother country was then emerging from prolonged civil war. Charles I had been executed. Oliver Cromwell, in command of the victorious parliamentary forces, was about to be made Protector of England, Scotland, and Ireland. Thus, although the Massachusetts colonists had no legal right to make coins, the British were too busy at home to police such matters.

Massachusetts was the principal trading colony in America and its growing merchant fleet was engaged in foreign and domestic commerce. Small coins were particularly needed for use within the colony, where the worn and depreciated foreign currency was becoming a nuisance. The General Court of Massachusetts authorized a mint to be set up in Boston, and John Hull, the mintmaster, made the coins from silver received principally from the colony's West Indian trade. To keep the coins within the colonial borders, they were made of 22 per cent less silver than current English coins of the same denominations, though the English standard of fineness—that is, the proportionate amount of silver in the coins—was preserved. Despite this precaution and rigid vigilance against shipment of the pieces to points outside Massachusetts, many of the coins soon found a welcome in other colonies and countries. English merchants accepted them, but raised prices of their goods to offset the reduced silver content.

The Massachusetts coins (figure 7a) were struck in twopenny, threepenny, sixpenny, and shilling denominations and are of four general types. All but the first type bear the emblem of a tree, and these are often referred to as the "tree" coins. More often they are called "Pine Tree" coins because of the pine on the last and largest issue.

*Figure 7. (a) Massachusetts "Pine Tree" shilling. (b) Lord Baltimore shilling.* (American Numismatic Society)

The first issue, consisting of threepenny, sixpenny, and shilling pieces, was rather crude. It simply had the letters NE (New England) on one side, and the denomination in Roman numerals on the other. It had no date and could easily be counterfeited. The second issue, the "Willow Tree," followed with more elaborate design. It featured the tree emblem with the word MASATHVSETS on one side, and the date, a beaded circle, and the words NEW ENGLAND on the other. Next came the "Oak Tree" issue, with an outer beaded circle to render clipping more easily detectable. Finally the "Pine Tree" coins appeared. They are believed to have been issued from about

1667 to 1682. All the tree coins are dated 1652, except for the twopenny piece, dated 1662.

After the restoration of the English monarchy in 1660, the Crown apparently allowed the coinage until the early 1680's. Although the General Court made a "present" to His Majesty of ten barrels of cranberries, two hogsheads of "special good sampe" (an Indian preparation of unhusked corn), and three thousand codfish, the king put a stop to the coinage about 1682.

Mintmaster Hull became a very rich man, since he received 15 pence for every 20 shillings' worth of coins he minted. The story is told that when his daughter married Samuel Sewall, Hull gave as her dowry her weight in New England shillings. Since one account reports that he gave Sewall thirty thousand, the daughter must have had ample proportions.

MARYLAND COINAGE

Maryland's right to coin money was not specified in the founding charter, issued in 1632 to Cecilius Calvert, the second Lord Baltimore. Nonetheless, he believed that he had this sovereign right, and he acted on the matter a quarter of a century later. Tobacco, the principal money of the colony, was overproduced and becoming increasingly unsatisfactory. He therefore had samples of proposed coinage struck in England and sent to the colony. At first the authorities of the colonial government in America strove to act independently of Lord Baltimore and to have the coins made in the colony. After considerable dickering Lord Baltimore prevailed and the coins (figure 7b) were issued in England in 1659 for distribution in Maryland.

The shilling, sixpence, and fourpence (groat) denominations were struck in silver, and the penny, called a "denarium," in copper. The silver coins were only about 75 per cent pure silver, much less than corresponding English coins. On the face of the coins was the bust of Calvert, and on the reverse side the Baltimore family arms, with the motto CRESCITE ET MULTIPLICAMINI (Increase and Be Multiplied). The reverse of the penny showed a small crown with two pennants and the inscription DENARIUM TER-RAEMARIAE (Maryland Penny).

According to Maryland laws of 1662, every "tithable" person was to exchange sixty pounds of tobacco, at a set price of 2 pence a pound, for 10 shillings in the new money. Though forced upon the colonists, the new coins proved useful and are also believed to have been profitable for Lord Baltimore. Though many of them were made, they are scarce today. The penny is especially rare.

IRISH COINS IN NEW JERSEY

Mystery surrounds the origin and exact date of issue of the St. Patrick pieces (figure 8) that appeared in New Jersey in the early 1680's. These silver and copper halfpenny and farthing coins are believed to have

*Figure 8. (a) St. Patrick three-farthing piece. (b) St. Patrick halfpenny. (c) Rosa Americana two-pence piece, 1722.* (American Numismatic Society)

been minted in Dublin for circulation in Ireland. Whether they were minted much earlier for the use of Irish patriots, or only a few years before they were brought to America, nobody seems to know. They were brought over in 1681 by Mark Newby, an emigrant from Dublin. How he secured them is not known. In the colonial records of New Jersey the coins were referred to as "Mark Newby's halfpence, called St. Patrick halfpence," though many were farthing pieces.

The St. Patrick pieces were welcomed by the colony, where the General Assembly made them legal tender in 1682. They must have been plentiful, for they circulated throughout the colony and are less rare today than many other colonial coins. On the front of the coins is the figure of a crowned king kneeling and playing a harp, with the legend FLOREAT REX (May the King Prosper). The other side of the coin shows St. Patrick surrounded by people, with the words ECCE GREX (Behold the Flock).

### "ROSA AMERICANA" TOKENS

One of the few instances of England's authorization of coins expressly for its American colonies was the granting of a patent to an Englishman, William Wood, to make the "Rosa Americana" copper tokens (figure 8c) for "current money" in America. At the same time he was given a patent for minting similar "Hibernia" tokens for Ireland, but these were rejected by the Irish and subsequently sent to America.

Both of these issues originated not so much from King George I's desire to provide money needed by his more distant subjects as from his wish to please his mistress, the Duchess of Kendal, who figured prominently in the negotiations for the patents. The deal was apparently profitable for her and for Wood, as the issues were among the largest of the entire colonial period. The coins were attractive, but, as they had less weight than regular English coins of the same denominations, they were unpopular.

The Rosa Americana pieces were issued in half-penny, penny, and twopenny denominations for the years 1722, 1723, 1724, and 1733. They feature on the front the bust of the king. On the reverse is a full-blown rose, with the words ROSA AMERICANA UTILE DULCI (American Rose—the Useful with the Pleasant). The Irish coins featured a similar design, but on the reverse side they displayed a seated figure with a harp and the word HIBERNIA. They were issued in 1722, 1723, and 1724, only in halfpenny and farthing denominations. For political reasons they were extremely unpopular in Ireland. Their rejection there is said to have been hastened by the Irish satirist Jonathan Swift, whose "Drapier Letters" protested the terms on which the patents were given to Wood.

Besides the Rosa Americana tokens two other colonial coinage issues were authorized by the British government. The first of these, worth only 1/24th part of a real, was a pewter piece issued in 1688 during the brief reign of James II. The Spanish denomination was obviously chosen because of the common use of Spanish coins in the colonies, but there is no record of its circulation. The other authorized issue was that of the Virginia halfpenny, issued by George

III in 1773. Virginia was the only American colony which had been given the right to coin money by its charter in 1606. Though the colony made elaborate plans to exercise this right about 1645, nothing came of them except the halfpenny of more than a century later.

HIGLEY COPPERS IN CONNECTICUT

From 1737 to 1739 John Higley smelted ore from his private copper mine near Granby, Connecticut, made his own dies, and minted threepenny tokens of pure copper. Though England had forbidden smelting in the colonies—all ore had to be shipped to England—it seems that nobody bothered Higley. He coined with no authority but his own, and the mine was a very profitable venture. (Higley's mine is not to be confused with a nearby copper mine which during the American Revolution served as Newgate Prison.)

The story is told that Higley's shiny new tokens, which displayed on one side THE VALUE OF THREE PENCE, were at first readily accepted by the local tavern he frequented. But when the bartender's till became full of the tokens, he refused to accept any more, saying that they were not real or legal money. Higley, undaunted by the rebuff, changed the tokens to read on one side VALUE ME AS YOU PLEASE and on the other I AM GOOD COPPER. Whether this revision made the pieces more acceptable or not, is not known. Today they are quite rare.

PROMOTIONAL COINS

A few issues of copper coins for advertising purposes were made privately in England for use in America. Among these were the "Gloucester" tokens of 1714 and the Carolina and New England "Elephant" tokens of 1694. The Gloucester piece was thought to have been made for use in Virginia. During the last half of the seventeenth century a "New Yorke" token appeared, the exact origin of which is unknown; it was the earliest coin for American use with the eagle design. In 1766 in Philadelphia tokens were issued by a Mr. Smithers to honor William Pitt the elder. This English statesman had fought for repeal of the Stamp Act that Britain had imposed on the colonies. This and similar acts eventually led to the American Revolution.

# 5

# PAPER MONEY TO WIN A WAR

Even though this history deals with coins, it cannot entirely ignore other contemporary forms of currency. Some of these have at times almost completely replaced coins or greatly affected their use. We have already seen how commodity money was used in place of coins during the colonial period. Once again, during five of the seven years of armed conflict known as the American Revolution, the people carried on almost completely without metallic money. At that critical time, paper money temporarily replaced the coins in circulation. This money, in the form of bills of credit, was known as Continental currency because it was issued by the Continental Congress. So much paper money was printed that people were unwilling to exchange their coins for the overvalued bills. They took their hard money out of circulation until conditions changed to favor the American cause near the end of the war. Meanwhile, the value of paper money fell, at first slowly, then rapidly, until it eventually became worthless. "Not worth a Continental" is an old American expression that is applied even today to something worth little or nothing.

BACKGROUND OF PAPER MONEY

The colonies had begun to use paper currency or bills of exchange long before the Revolution. In 1690 Massachusetts issued paper money in order to pay the expenses of a military expedition against the French in Canada. These bills are considered by some to have been the first such government-backed money in the British Empire. They proved a great convenience in the emergency and were later redeemed out of revenues from taxation.

Other paper issues followed later in Massachusetts (figure 9) and in nearly all of the colonies. Sometimes the results were satisfactory, but often users of the currency lost money. Such losses usually resulted from overproduction of the notes, followed by a failure to redeem them promptly—or at all—in coin. So great, however, was the need for money in the growing colonies that continued use of paper currency was justified by such leaders as Benjamin Franklin, though he cautioned against overproduction. Some of the colonial governors also defended paper money, although the British government, which they represented, had early taken a stand against it.

Finally, in 1741, the British Parliament forbade

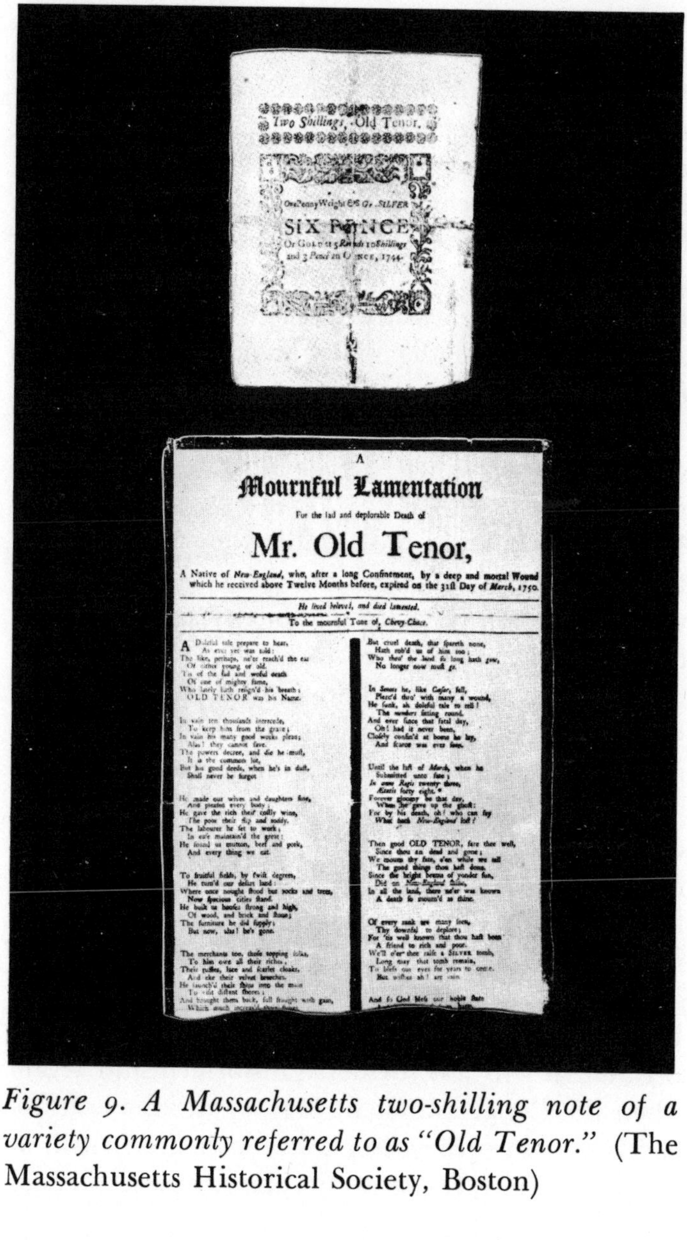

*Figure 9. A Massachusetts two-shilling note of a variety commonly referred to as "Old Tenor."* (The Massachusetts Historical Society, Boston)

further issuance of paper money in New England, and in 1764 extended this prohibition to all the colonies. The British Board of Trade argued that both British merchants and the colonists themselves had suffered because paper currency tended to drive gold and silver money out of the colonies. Nevertheless, the colonies greatly resented the British currency ruling, and the move became an important factor in the discontent leading to the Revolution.

### WHY AND HOW PAPER MONEY WAS USED IN THE WAR

When the war began the colonies were at a disadvantage financially, as well as in other respects. With a total population estimated at about 2.5 million, they had no strong, centralized form of government and no common treasury. The Continental Congress, which directed the war, was merely a loosely bound assemblage of delegates from the various colonies, with no power to tax or to impose other levies. Nevertheless, the body could direct colonial opinion by making resolutions and recommendations calling for united action. Thus, in September 1774, at the first meeting of the Congress, in Philadelphia, the delegates set in motion a boycott against trade with England.

Colonial will was further transformed into action when the Congress met in May 1775, after warfare had begun in earnest in clashes with the British at Lexington and Concord in Massachusetts. There was much argument at the Congress on how the colonies were to pay for the rapidly growing army and meet other expenses. Without money of its own or the ability to tax, the Congress decided that issuing paper money was the best way out of the dilemma. This money (figure 10) was backed by "the Resolution of the Congress" of the "United Colonies," pledging the faith of all the colonies to redeem the bills in "Spanish milled dollars." Congress specified that the colonies should do this over a four-year period, between 1779 and 1782, in amounts corresponding to their respective populations. Since Congress lacked the authority to compel acceptance of the Continental notes, more commonly known as "Continentals," each of the states responded by making them legal tender. Penalties were set by the colonies and the Congress for anyone refusing to accept the bill in payment. Such refusal by a person would result in his forfeiture of a debt owed to him, or in his being branded "an enemy of the country."

The first issue of the bills, authorized June 22, 1775, was a relatively modest one of $2 million, in denominations ranging from $1 to $20. This was followed by $4 million printed that year. From 1776 on, however, the issues were of far greater amounts, in response to the pressure of unfavorable events and the need of more money for waging the war. By 1779 the various issues had reached the astounding total of about $241 million.

At first, while hope remained that the bills would

The United States.

Twenty Dollars. No. 7 1116

This BILL entitles the Bearer to receive TWENTY SPANISH MILLED DOLLARS, or the Value thereof in Gold or Silver, according to a Resolution, passed by Congress at Philadelphia, Sept. 26th, 1778.

VI. CONCITATÆ.

XX DOLLARS.

TWENTY DOLLARS.

Printed by HALL and SELLERS. 1778.

be redeemed in coin, they were accepted at face value. But in 1776, when excessive printing of the money began, confidence in it faded rapidly. Numerous steps were taken to stop the depreciation in value of the currency, which was causing higher and higher prices for everything purchased. But efforts made to make the various states redeem their paper money quotas or make loans to Congress to carry on the war were in vain, for Congress did not have the power to enforce such measures. After the Declaration of Independence, July 4, 1776, the heading "United States" replaced that of "United Colonies" on Continental currency. At times this bold title seemed an empty boast.

By early 1779 the value of the paper dollar had dropped to 3 cents. Since it seemed likely to become worthless, Congress stopped printing the bills later that year. Indeed, they did become practically worthless when the states began to cancel the legal-tender status of the money. Even the Congress finally agreed to this move. Realizing the futility of printing more money, Revolutionary leaders had to seek other means of financing the conflict.

TRAGIC RESULTS OF INFLATION
Though perhaps no more than 40 per cent of the American people actively supported the Revolution,

*Figure 10. Continental currency, twenty dollars.* (American Numismatic Society)

the downfall of the Continental bills affected the vast majority. There were ruinous losses for rich and poor alike, for debts contracted for good money were paid off with almost valueless currency. Meanwhile, speculators and other unscrupulous persons profited by the situation. In patriot territory prominent leaders were sometimes suspected of profiteering and of fraudulent dealings in handling the money or supplies. Sometimes riots resulted, as in Philadelphia late in 1779 under the very eyes of the Congress in session.

For the British and their Tory allies, however, it was a time of rejoicing. They easily foresaw victory for the king's forces. To hasten the decline of the rebel fortunes, British-occupied New York was made a center for counterfeiting large quantities of the American money. Meanwhile, behind the British lines, coins paid by the British to their troops and to local farmers for food circulated freely. Some found their way outside to aid the American cause. Nevertheless, late 1779 and 1780 saw this cause threatened with bankruptcy and extinction. It was the gloomiest period of the Revolution.

STATE SUPPORT AND CURRENCY

From the various states, which often supported the Congress only grudgingly, limited food and other supplies came to the Continental Army under General George Washington. In fact, many of the forces in the conflict consisted of troops raised, equipped, and supported by separate states. The states also printed paper money in large amounts throughout the Revolutionary period, especially in the 1780's, after the Continental issues had been stopped. In the states it was considered easier to finance the war by printing paper money than by imposing taxes, which were generally unpopular. Some of this paper money became as worthless as the Continental bills, but on the whole its depreciation was less severe. In some states, notably in Connecticut and Delaware, its value held up remarkably well. The practice of printing state money was prohibited in 1789, when the Constitution of the United States was adopted.

FRENCH AID

During America's darkest hours hope came from French financial and military assistance. After the defeat of the British army under Burgoyne at Saratoga in the fall of 1777, France saw the possibility of a final American victory and signed an alliance with the fledgling nation early in 1778. French military aid proved decisive in the defeat of the British at Yorktown, Virginia, in October 1781. France is estimated to have supplied about $8 million in loans and subsidies, not including about $1 million advanced before its entry into the war. Much of this money came in the form of badly needed gold and silver coin. Considerable cash also came from Holland and Spain, the latter then an ally of France. The loans from these three nations were later to be repaid when the new nation was financially solvent.

Coins that had been in hiding now entered circulation along with the new hard money from abroad, so that for several years after 1780 the American people had a relatively good supply of gold and silver coin. Among the pieces in circulation were many Portuguese "joes" and "half-joes," Spanish doubloons, and English and French guineas. The outlook for the American people had improved greatly, but during the period between the end of the war and the establishment of the federal government in 1789 there was no firm control over the many and often debased currencies in circulation. In this period of instability and change, trial and error, the state governments reluctantly gave way to a centralized authority, that of the United States.

An important step in this direction was taken when the nation's first constitution, the Articles of Confederation, was ratified in 1781. It limited the independence of the individual states and gave some significant powers to the Continental Congress, which became known as the Congress of the Confederation. The Articles guaranteed the privileges of citizens in any state into which they moved and gave Congress exclusive control over international relations. And, though Congress still could not impose taxes, it could borrow money, issue paper money, and fix the value of money coined by it and the states.

The Revolution had been won and the Continental paper bills, now virtually worthless, were still to be found in households as bitter reminders of the sacrifices the people had made during the war. Stories traveled around about a barber who papered his shop with the old notes, and about the sailors who made suits by cutting the notes up and pasting them together. Although losses from use of the paper currency were heavy and often unfairly distributed, the currency had helped greatly in winning the war.

# 6

# SEPARATE COINS FOR SEPARATE STATES

The period between the end of the war and the establishment of the United States under the Constitution was politically unstable. As one result, the currency was disorganized. Many kinds of copper coins were experimented with. Although the return to peacetime brought back into the avenues of trade foreign gold and silver currency that had disappeared during the war, the great need for "small change" coins soon became evident. This need caught the attention of eager suppliers of such coins with special force. Never before had the American people dealt with such a wide variety of coins.

### INFLUX OF COPPERS

Numerous copper cent and halfpenny pieces began to appear from various sources. Some were issued by states with the consent of the Congress of the Confederation, then the only form of national government. Congress itself issued experimental or pattern pieces from time to time, but most of the coppers were minted for profit by private coiners in England and in the states. These pieces were mostly of "base" metallic mixtures, low in copper content and therefore in intrinsic value. They became an increasing cause of complaints and dissatisfaction and were a factor in hastening the advent of our national coinage system.

It has been estimated that some $10 million in coins of all types moved into circulation in 1782 and 1783. Between the latter year and 1785, however, because of a temporarily unfavorable trade balance in the flow of products between America and Europe, a large number of the coins were exported. Panic swept the commercial centers until America's trade position improved in 1785, and coins began to return to circulation.

STATE COINS

Many of the state copper coins were issued in the late 1780's, not only with the idea of providing better coins in place of the "base coppers" that continued to pour into the country, but also with the hope that coins minted in America would stay in the country.

New Hampshire was the first state to consider a coinage of its own in the Revolutionary period. It authorized halfpenny-size copper pieces to be struck in 1776, but only a few pattern pieces (proposed new designs for regular coinage) were actually made.

It remained for Vermont, beginning in 1785, to

provide the first postwar copper issue, a 1-cent denomination (figure 11a). A rather primitive mint at Rupert made the coins by means of an iron screw attached to heavy timbers above and moved by hand with the aid of ropes. Most of the pieces were struck in the patterns of existing halfpenny and other current copper coins, and they were dated from 1785 to 1788.

Connecticut's issue of copper cent pieces (figure 11b) during the same years was one of the largest of any state. Some twenty-nine thousand pounds of copper were used to make the pieces of standard British halfpenny weight. One-twentieth part of the amount coined by contracting coiners was paid into the state's treasury.

Massachusetts, between 1786 and 1788, also produced a large quantity of cent and half-cent copper pieces (figure 11c) at its own mint in Boston. The venture was unprofitable and was finally abandoned in 1789. Originally it was planned that the mint would turn out gold and silver coins, but these were never produced. The Massachusetts cent was valued at 1/100th of the Spanish dollar, and is thus considered the first official coin in history based strictly on a decimal system. According to Commonwealth records, a large amount of the metal for both the cent and half-cent pieces came from melting down a number of brass cannon and other armaments of high copper content.

In 1786 New Jersey granted to Thomas Goadsby,

*Figure 11.* (a) *Vermont one-cent piece, 1788.* (b)
*Connecticut cent, 1788.* (c) *Massachusetts copper
cent, 1787.* (d) *New Jersey copper cent, 1786.*
(American Numismatic Society)

Albion Cox, and Walter Mould the authority to coin a large quantity of copper cent pieces (figure 11d), on condition that they deliver to the state's treasury "one-tenth part of the full sum they shall strike and coin." Two mints were operated, one at Morristown, the other at Elizabethtown. Their owners were, respectively, Mould, formerly a coiner in Birmingham, England, and Cox, who probably had Goadsby as a partner. The Cox mill was operated by Gilbert Rindle. The cents minted often bore the legend NOVA CAESAREA (New Jersey), with the emblem of a horse and plow on the face. On the reverse was a shield with the legend E PLURIBUS UNUM, later adopted for use on U.S. coins.

The majority of state coins were made in the northeastern section of the country, where commerce, industry, and large centers of population generally required greatest use of them. Each state, however, had postwar coppers in circulation. Some of these were authorized in neighboring states and even struck, both by official mints and private coiners, outside the state of their origin. For instance, many of the official Connecticut and New Jersey cents, issued in great quantities, circulated in other states, particularly in neighboring ones.

PRIVATE COIN AND TOKEN ISSUES

Although New York had no official state coinage, a large number and variety of cent pieces, as well as many different tokens, were made by private coiners in the state. They generally bore 1786 and 1787 dates. One of the principal private operations was at Machin's Mill near Newburgh. This enterprise, called a "manufactory of hardware," was said to have been conducted largely in secrecy and was regarded by some as illegal. It has been observed that perhaps a number of coppers classified as Connecticut and Vermont coins were actually produced at Machin's Mill.

New York was one of the biggest centers for the distribution of inferior copper coins during the period. Commercial firms in New York City and in other large Atlantic seaboard cities reaped big profits by buying the coins in England and putting them into circulation in America. The Americans were only too willing to accept them as good coins, giving little thought to their actual worth. The user had no way of getting back what he had paid for them, for they bore the name of neither the originator nor the promoter responsible for them. Generally they were not coins, but only tokens which passed for coins, and eventually were looked on as worthless. Still, they tended to drive good money out of circulation. Many of these pieces were struck at the mint of Matthew Boulton in Birmingham, England. This was true of a token struck in honor of Kentucky in 1792, when it became the fifteenth state. As Sylvester Crosby points out in *The Early Coins of America,* "Most of the specimens known as New York coppers are of English origin, and entitled to that name, if at all, only from the fact that they bear devices and legends indicating that they were circulated in New York State."

Realizing that its people were being fleeced by the influx of inferior pieces, the New York State Legislature in 1787 passed a rigid law to stop their use. The law stated that "no coppers shall pass current in this state, except such as are of standard weight of one-third part of an ounce of pure copper, which shall pass at the rate of 20 to a shilling of lawful current money in the state." It was further specified that persons who knowingly passed the overvalued coins "shall forfeit five times the value of the sum for which the coppers shall be offered or passed in payment, to be recovered before any justice of the peace." In 1778 the state passed a law against counterfeiters caught making debased or illegal coins. Those found guilty would suffer the death penalty.

Pennsylvania, Rhode Island, and New Jersey passed similar restrictive measures against the influx of debased coins. But laws of this kind were generally ineffective. They came too late, after the damage had been done of flooding the country with inferior money.

WASHINGTON PIECES

Private coiners of the postwar period quite naturally sought to honor General Washington. Many of the English-made coppers, as well as some struck in America, bore the general's portrait, often in very

*Figure 12.* (a) *Washington and Independence, 1783.*
(b) *Washington half dollar, 1792.* (American Numismatic Society)

good likenesses. A number of the pieces emphasized
patriotic themes, such as the desire for unity among
the states and their striving for nationhood (figure
12a). The American eagle, later featured on U.S.
coins, was used on certain of the private Washington
issues, some of which were struck after the general
became President (figure 12b). Although no denomination is indicated on many of these pieces,
the word CENT appears on some. There are also
halfpenny denominations and even half-dollar copper pieces. The latter may have been intended as
patterns for the silver half dollar later officially is-

sued by the United States, though Washington's image did not appear on the coin finally adopted.

PRIVATE GOLD AND SILVER PIECES

A few gold and silver pieces were privately struck in the postwar period. The most famous and desirable of these was the gold doubloon struck in 1787 by Ephraim Brasher, a New York goldsmith. Worth $16 at that time, the few remaining specimens are now among the rarest American numismatic items. In 1783, in Maryland, John Chalmers, an Annapolis goldsmith, made silver tokens of threepenny, six-penny, and shilling denominations.

A national coinage for the American people was greatly delayed for several reasons. The principal one, of course, was that Americans were too busy fighting a war for independence during the early years of nationhood. Another was that the need of the Continental Congress to finance the conflict with paper money resulted in driving coins from circulation. Moreover, the respective states had been accustomed to playing an independent role in money matters. A number of the states had been issuing coins or paper money or both for generations and continued to issue money of their own after the war. The states were reluctant to delegate this authority to a national government in process of development. It was a difficult transition and it took time.

# 7

# THE SHAPING
# OF A NATIONAL
# COINAGE SYSTEM

As early as 1776 some thought had been given to the establishment of a national coinage. That year the first U.S. silver-dollar-size coin, the Continental-currency piece referred to as the "Continental dollar," was issued. The pieces, struck in pewter and brass as well as silver, are thought to have been patterns or trial pieces for a coinage that failed to materialize. Mystery, however, surrounds their origin. There seems to be no record of who coined them or where they were minted. Some believe that Congress had a hand in their creation, though definite proof of this is lacking. At any rate, the designs on the Continental-currency coinage are derived from the Continental paper notes of February 17, 1776. The pieces were made from dies on which the initials E. G. were engraved. This was possibly Elisha Gallaudet, a New York engraver.

On the face of the dollar are featured the words CONTINENTAL CURRENCY; the design of the sundial

*Figure 13. (a) Continental dollar, 1776. (b) Copper
cent, "Nova Constellatio," 1783. (c) Fugio cent,
1787. Right: (d, e, f) "Nova Constellatio" silver pattern pieces proposed by Gouverneur and Robert
Morris and designed by Benjamin Dudley in 1783
—mark, quint, and bit.* (C. H. Weber, Johns Hop-
kins University)

and nearby the word FUGIO, interpreted to mean that time is fleeing; and underneath the warning MIND YOUR BUSINESS (figure 13a). On the reverse of the coin appears a chain of thirteen links around the circumference, each link representing one of the original thirteen states, and also the legend AMERI-CAN CONGRESS and WE ARE ONE (figure 13b). The designs of the coin are quite similar to those which appeared on the Fugio cent of 1787, described later in this chapter.

SEARCH FOR A COINAGE SYSTEM
An organized attempt to establish a national coinage

system began in the early 1780's and lasted for about a decade before the U.S. Mint was finally founded in 1792. This slow, tedious process reflected the difficulties of the transition from the relatively weak government under the Articles of Confederation to the stronger and more centralized authority of the federal government under the Constitution. Fortunately, however, the country was blessed with such able leaders as Robert Morris, Gouverneur Morris, Thomas Jefferson, and Alexander Hamilton, all of whom contributed to the establishment of the nation's coinage system.

Studies which led to the earliest proposals for a national coinage system began under the direction of Robert Morris, well known as "the financier of the Revolution." It was he who had somehow raised the money to enable General Washington to move the Continental Army south to Yorktown, Virginia, in 1781, where the final battle of the war was won. Morris had been made superintendent of finance by the Congress of the Confederation. In 1782 that body directed him to prepare a report on the values of foreign coins then circulating in the states, with the idea of drawing up a plan for a national coinage system. Work on the report, however, was left largely in the hands of Morris' able helper, the assistant superintendent of finance, Gouverneur Morris. Gouverneur Morris, who was not related to Robert Morris, was a New York financier then in Philadelphia, where Congress was meeting.

One of the major problems was to prepare a coinage system with units or denominations of money that would be exchangeable with the existing coins in circulation. As visualized, it would be a system that would take into account the different values of coins in various states and sections of the country. Yet the new denominations would be entirely unlike any of the coins in use.

The Spanish dollar, still regarded as the standard monetary unit of the country, continued to have four different valuations in different sections of the country. Expressed in pence, the dollar was variously valued at 60, 72, 90, and 96 pence. It was necessary that the proposed new U.S. coins should fit into this complicated situation, with the hope, of course, that they would eventually replace the existing coins.

The least common multiple of the four different dollar valuations was 1440. That was almost exactly the number of one-quarter grains of pure silver in the Spanish dollar. So it was considered that the smallest division of the new coinage would be a "unit" or "quarter," that is, 1/1440th of the dollar. This amount, of course, would be too small for a coin. It was somewhat comparable to the mill, later adopted as the nation's smallest accounting unit, but never represented by a coin.

The largest silver coin proposed by the Morrises was the "mark," valued at 1,000 units, worth about 73 per cent of the Spanish dollar. Next there would be the "quint," valued at 500 units and worth about

36.5 cents, and the "cent," also a silver coin, valued at 100 units and worth about 7 cents. The next smaller denominations would be copper pieces, the "eight" or eight units, and the "five" or five units. The latter pieces would be worth about ½ cent and ⅓ cent respectively.

It was pointed out by supporters of this coinage that any ordinary transaction in either Spanish or English money could be carried out in terms of the new units or quarters. It was both a clever and revolutionary system, especially in that it marked the beginning of a decimal coinage system. (Only the two small copper coins, the five and the eight, were not decimal denominations.) But the proposed system had flaws, which critics soon pointed out. As a decimal system, for example, it did not have any coin valued at 1/100th of a mark, comparable to the present cent in relation to the dollar. Also the five coin was considered too small for practical use.

FIRST PATTERN COINS

Nevertheless, Congress gave its approval to the report submitted by the Morrises, and asked them to produce samples of the proposed coins for further study. Such samples, usually called "pattern" coins, are produced in limited number by any country contemplating a new coinage. From such samples the best-liked may become models for regular coins-to-be. Benjamin Dudley, an Englishman whom Gouverneur Morris had met in Boston, was called upon to design the new pieces proposed by the Morrises, and these were struck bearing the date 1783. They included the silver mark, two types of the silver quint, the silver cent, and possibly the two copper pieces. Only meager records are available concerning production of all these pieces.

Only one specimen each of the mark and the quint are known to exist, and only two known specimens of the silver pattern piece (figure 13). These coins are classified in coin books as "Nova Constellatio" patterns, because they bear on their faces the words NOVA CONSTELLATIO (a new constellation, or group of stars), evidently to represent the new states becoming a nation. On the reverse of the pieces the letters U.S. are centered. Beneath them the numerals 1,000, 500, and 100 respectively indicate the denominations. No patterns of the smaller denomination (copper) pieces are known to exist today.

It has been pointed out in numismatic works on the period that the original coinage plan devised by the Morrises was to have been primarily concerned with silver coins, possibly with the intention of adopting for the new nation a single silver standard. Later, however, as studies of the proposal progressed, revised plans were presented by the two statesmen. These provided for gold as well as silver coins, and substituted new names for certain denominations previously proposed.

## THOMAS JEFFERSON'S PROPOSAL

Jefferson, who drew up a comprehensive plan of his own, also had a decisive influence in determining what kind of coins the United States would later use. Although he agreed with the Morrises' proposal for a decimal coinage, Jefferson thought the large silver coins should be more like the Spanish pieces the people had become accustomed to. He also wanted a double standard of coinage, consisting of gold and silver valued at the ratio of fifteen to one. That is, gold would be worth fifteen times as much as silver, a ratio believed to exist at that time in the world market. He urged that Congress choose a monetary unit equivalent to the Spanish dollar, with subdivisions on a strictly decimal basis.

The largest silver coin proposed by Jefferson was the "unit" or "dollar," containing 365 grains of pure silver (the amount he thought to be the approximate weight of the average Spanish dollar). Of proportional silver content would be the "half dollar" or "five tenths," the "fifth" or "pistareen," the "tenth" or "bit," and the "twentieth" or "half-bit," the smallest silver coin. As the coin of smallest value, Jefferson proposed a "hundredth" of copper, later called a cent. He also suggested a gold coin of ten units or dollars.

Except for relatively minor changes, it was Jefferson's plan that was finally adopted as the basis of our coinage system. Of course, it took more years of deliberation by Congressional committees and monetary experts before the details were worked out. Names of the denominations were changed and new denominations were added.

Both the Morris and Jefferson proposals were studied at length by a Congressional group known as the Grand Committee, which had representatives from each state. Jefferson's plan, based on the well-known Spanish coins then in use, had the advantage of simplicity. It could be better understood than the completely new kinds of coins proposed by Robert Morris.

Morris' main purpose was to produce a completely new U.S. money that would drive out and replace Spanish and other foreign coins. If he had been able to explain more clearly how his proposals would accomplish this aim he might have won. Morris pointed out that Jefferson's plan would not drive out the Spanish coins. Neither would it eliminate the Americans' habit of reckoning values in terms of English money. And as events turned out, Morris was right. But his explanation to Congress was so highly technical that it bewildered the delegates, who were not financial experts. They rejected Morris' system in favor of the proposal that Jefferson presented in his simple, lucid, and convincing language.

CONGRESSIONAL CHANGES

Before the favored plan was presented to Congress in May 1785, the Grand Committee had made a number of changes and additions, including the amount of metal the coins would contain. The committee also recommended that the government be allowed to make a 2 per cent seigniorage or profit. That is, each coin would bring the treasury 2 per cent more than the actual cost of metal and minting. The committee substituted a quarter dollar for Jefferson's fifth. (Much later, in 1875, the United States did finally issue a 20-cent silver piece as an experiment, but soon abandoned it as too much like the quarter in size and design.) They also proposed a new copper coin, the "two-hundredth," which was later called the half cent. This was a victory for Morris, who had objected that the hundredth, later known as the cent, had too large a value to be the smallest coin.

On July 6, 1785, Congress formally resolved that the nation's coinage system should be decimal, with the dollar as its standard unit. This was the first official adoption by any country of a decimal coinage system.

Robert Morris had resigned in 1784 from his assignment of working out plans for a mint. He was replaced in this task by a Board of Treasury. The board busied itself with a survey of the coinage problem and came up with some new names for already proposed coins. It decided that the $10 gold coin should feature the eagle emblem and be called an "eagle." Jefferson's tenth should be called a "disme" (later changed to dime). At the same time the word cent replaced the hundreth, and half cent the two-hundredth. It was decided, too, that our coinage system should have an accounting unit called the "mille," later spelled "mill," which still continues in use. It is worth 1/1000th of a dollar.

Following endorsement of the Board of Treasury's report in August 1786, Congress directed that body to prepare plans for a mint. In the following October it passed a mint ordinance. Certain provisions of this law quickly aroused considerable controversy. They provided that no foreign copper coins were to circulate within U.S. boundaries after September 1787, and that copper coins made by the states should have weights specified by Congress. The effect of the latter provision would have been to take the underweight state coins out of use. Strenuous objections came from those states which felt that they should continue to have certain privileges in coining money. They protested that the federal government was overreaching its authority. As a result, the mint ordinance became largely ineffective, and no mint was established at that time.

FUGIO CENTS

If undesirable copper coins were to be taken out of circulation, Congress had to find good copper substitutes. Such was the reasoning behind a resolution of 1787 providing for minting the famous Fugio cent (figure 13c), sometimes called the Franklin cent because its mottoes have been attributed to Benjamin Franklin. These were the first coins issued by the

United States government for general public use.

The Board of Treasury, having no national mint, was authorized to have the Fugios made privately. It was to contract for three hundred tons of copper of "federal standard." James Jarvis, a private coiner, was to provide a 15 per cent profit for the government, which could be applied to reducing the domestic debt. Though records do not reveal whether all of the proposed coins were struck, the issue was undoubtedly a considerable one for those times. The coins, many of which are still in collectors' hands, were made in New Haven, New York, and Rupert, Vermont. It is said that most of the metal used came from melting down items from military stores, such as copper bands that had held together powder kegs sent to the U.S. by the French during the Revolution.

In those days there were relatively few publications and none of the modern means of influencing public opinion, such as daily newspapers, radio, and television. Perhaps the Fugios, bearing Franklin's words of wisdom, helped to unify the people, as well as to provide them with more good coins. The slogan WE ARE ONE on the coins expressed hope for a unified government, a goal that was not yet fully realized.

The Congress of the Confederation represented a stronger union of the states than did the original Continental Congress. Nevertheless, the states were still reluctant to relinquish certain of their powers in order to create an effective central government.

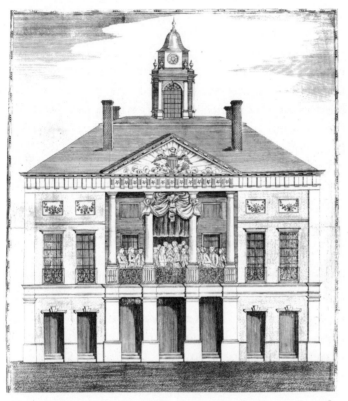

*Figure 14. Federal Hall, New York, in 1789, the seat of Congress.* (Stokes Collection, New York Public Library)

Not only were they reluctant to give up their long-enjoyed privileges of coining money, they also often quarreled over their respective boundaries and set up interstate tariff barriers. As a result of domestic disunity, foreign trade and relations deteriorated, and enemies of the infant nation predicted its early demise.

However, as the people and their leaders came to realize their predicament, the tide changed. In Congress this was expressed by the passage of the Northwest Ordinance of 1787, which provided for the creation of new states, under Congressional supervision, in the country's western territories. But it was the new Constitution, drafted in Philadelphia in 1787, that was of utmost importance in strengthening the central government. It established a national executive and gave Congress the power to regulate interstate commerce, to levy taxes, and to coin and borrow money. By July 1788 the Constitution had been ratified by eleven of the thirteen states, and preparations were made to inaugurate the new government in New York City on March 4, 1789 (figure 14). Postponed, the event actually took place on April 30, 1789.

# 8

# THE FOUNDING
# OF OUR MINT

A new nation has a lot to think about when it starts
"from scratch" to produce the coins destined to be
its perennial calling cards in the world of trade. Men
versed in law and science must determine the makeup and use of the currency. The works of art, em-
blems, and slogans chosen to adorn the coins should
express some of the cherished beliefs of the nation's
people.

ESTABLISHMENT OF LAWS AND POLICIES
Preliminary steps in shaping the coinage system had
been worked out by the Morrises, Jefferson, the
Grand Committee, and the Board of Treasury under
the government of the Confederation. But it was
Alexander Hamilton, the young and able first Secretary of the Treasury, who had the task of establishing
the U.S. Mint and making the coinage system sound
and workable. He included important recommendations in his report to Congress in 1791 on the establishment of the mint. This report served as the basis

of the Coinage Act of April 1792, officially entitled "An Act Establishing a Mint and Regulating the Coins of the United States."

According to the act, the dollar would be the nation's monetary unit, defined in terms of both gold and silver, with gold valued fifteen times as high as silver. The act specified that "the money of account of the United States should be expressed in dollars or units, dismes or tenths, cents or hundredths, and milles or thousandths; a disme being the tenth part of a dollar, a cent the hundredth part of a dollar, a mille the thousandth part of a dollar."

Denominations were defined in the act as follows:

| | Value | Grains pure * | Grains standard * |
|---|---|---|---|
| Gold Eagle | $10.00 | 247 4/8 | 270 |
| Gold Half Eagle | 5.00 | 123 6/8 | 135 |
| Gold Quarter Eagle | 2.50 | 61 7/8 | 67 4/8 |
| Silver Dollar | 1.00 | 371 4/16 | 416 |
| Silver Half Dollar | .50 | 185 10/16 | 208 |
| Silver Quarter Dollar | .25 | 92 13/16 | 104 |
| Silver Disme | .10 | 37 2/16 | 41 3/5 |
| Silver Half Disme | .05 | 18 9/16 | 20 4/5 |
| Copper Cent | .01 | 11 pwt [264 gr] | |
| Copper Half Cent | .005 | 5 1/2 pwt [132 gr] | |

* "Grains pure" denotes the amount of pure gold or silver in the coin. "Grains standard" is the total weight with alloy mixed in. The copper coins contained only pure copper.

The fineness of the silver coins, according to the specifications, would be 892.43. In other words, the proportion of pure silver in a coin was to be 11/12th. The remaining 1/12th was an alloy added to the pure metal to improve the wearing qualities of the coin. The gold coins would be 916.67 fine, since they needed less alloy than the silver pieces. The copper coins would be of pure copper.

Hamilton was a firm believer in coins of high intrinsic value. He deplored any form of debasement that would reduce the pure metal content of a coin to much less than its money value. This philosophy was to cause many currency difficulties later on, because the supply and prices of metals from which coins are made fluctuate and this affects their circulation and usage.

Passage of the Coinage Act of 1792 was not an easy task. As already noted, some opponents of the measure did not want the federal government to take over coinage functions long enjoyed by the individual states. Many people still considered the Spanish currency satisfactory. The act barely passed Congress by a vote of twenty-five to twenty-one.

A monumental achievement of the Coinage Act, reflecting the foresight and planning behind it, was that most of the denominations listed in it survived for many years. The list includes most of the coins still in use, although changes were necessarily made from time to time in their design and metal content. Coinage of the half cent was stopped in 1857, but the half dollar, the quarter, the dime, and the cent still remain. The 5-cent nickel, too, is of the same denominational value as the original half dime, which continued to be minted until 1873. And though the silver dollar has largely disappeared in recent years, it is still a familiar coin. All gold coins were removed from circulation in 1933.

In determining what the weight of the silver dollar should be, Hamilton measured a random assortment of the then current Spanish dollars and found their average pure silver content to be 371¼ grains. That weight was established for the silver dollar, and its proportional fractions for the smaller silver pieces.

European estimates of the value of gold and silver were said to be the basis of Jefferson's and Hamilton's belief that gold was fifteen times more valuable than silver. Thus, the pure gold equivalent of the dollar unit was fixed at 24⅔ grains. The United States did not actually mint a gold dollar, however, until 1849.

Defining the dollar in terms of both gold and silver, without favoring the use of one metal over the other, later came to be known as the "double standard" or bimetallism. Many experts believe that it was a serious mistake to adopt the double standard. It was very difficult to maintain it, for metal prices continually changed, affecting the established ratio of 15 to 1. It was soon discovered that gold had been undervalued at this ratio, but the country had to wait until 1834 for gold to be given a 16 to 1 ratio.

The problem was eventually solved by adopting the single gold standard in 1873, but a bitter conflict over the matter of gold and silver coinage raged for three decades thereafter.

For the sake of economy, Hamilton wanted fewer coins than the Coinage Act finally called for. He thought, for example, that it was best to have at first only two silver denominations, the dollar and the dime. The intermediate pieces—the half dollar, quarter, and half dime—could be included later, as they were needed. But Congress overruled him.

Under the Coinage Act, the cent would have been an inconveniently large coin containing 264 grains of copper. Hamilton agreed that it should be reduced in size. But, disapproving of any debasement of the coinage, he believed that its intrinsic value should be maintained by including a trace of silver in its composition. Instead, in January 1793, before any coppers had been minted, Congress reduced the copper cent from 264 grains to 208 grains, and the half cent in proportion, but they did not agree to add the silver. This reduction, the Congress maintained, would give the government a "reasonable profit" and help defray the heavy expense of operating the mint. This earliest inflationary step in our coinage was bitterly criticized, some calling it "legal robbery." Nevertheless, late in 1795, the cent was further reduced to 168 grains and remained at that size until 1857, when the large copper piece was replaced by the smaller copper-nickel cent. Considered a minor coinage, the coppers were never made legal tender, as were gold and silver pieces. But, as in the past, copper coins continued to be important in making change and in small purchases.

### THE PROBLEM OF FOREIGN COINS

The Coinage Act of 1792 specified that all U.S. gold and silver coins should have unlimited legal-tender status, and that worn coins should be legal tender with values proportionate to their weight in pure metal content. The act failed, however, to provide for redemption of badly worn coins, which were primarily Spanish, though Hamilton, like Robert Morris, visualized the gradual elimination of all foreign coins.

Early in 1793, however, the law was amended to deal with the legal-tender status of all foreign coins, somewhat along the lines recommended by Hamilton. It provided that three years after the beginning of gold and silver coinage at the mint, foreign coins, except the Spanish silver pieces, would no longer be legal tender. Moreover, after the start of mint operations, all foreign gold and silver pieces received by the government as money due it, except the Spanish dollar and its parts, were to be melted and recoined as U.S. money.

Worthy as the purpose of the law might be in favoring domestic coinage, its enforcement was impossible. For sixty-four years afterward, foreign coins were a dwindling but important part of the coins in circulation because domestic coins failed to supply the nation's needs.

ESTABLISHMENT OF THE MINT

The U.S. Mint was established in Philadelphia, then the nation's capital, in 1792 (figure 15). President Washington was instrumental in purchasing its site, a plot of ground on Seventh Street between Market and Arch streets, because he was greatly interested in the project. The small brick building was said to be the first public structure built by the new government. The machinery and facilities for making coins were limited. Horsepower was used in rolling out the metal into thin sheets. These were later cut into strips from which planchets or blanks could be punched and then stamped into coins by hand-operated presses.

Although the first regular issues of coins (figure 16) from the mint were the cent and half-cent pieces struck in 1793, the first coins actually made at the establishment, even before its construction was completed, were a small quantity of half dimes (or dismes, as they were originally called) in October 1792. It is said that President Washington supplied some of the silver needed for producing these pieces from his own private silverware. A small sample issue of the first dimes was also struck at about this time. The first regular issue of half dimes, however, did not come from the mint until 1794, the year the first dollars and half dollars were struck. Dimes and

Figure 15. (a) First United States Mint at Philadelphia, 1792. (b) The mint as it appears today. (Chase
Manhattan Bank Collection, Moneys of the World)

quarters were not regularly issued until 1796, and the first gold coins—$5 half eagles and $10 eagles—appeared in 1795. Delays in minting the silver and gold issues were caused by the inability of the assayer and chief coiner of the new mint to furnish immediately the required security bond of $10,000. Robert Scot was the first engraver. David Rittenhouse, the first director of the mint, was in charge of all its operations.

FREE COINAGE

According to the law, people were entitled to have their gold and silver made into U.S. coins at the mint free of charge. This English custom was thought to be a means of rapidly increasing production and the amount of coins in circulation. The cost of coinage was therefore absorbed by the government. If the person furnishing the metal wanted the coins immediately, however, he would be charged ½ per cent of the total value of the coins, deducted before delivery.

Because of the limited facilities for producing coins and the relatively high cost of operations, the inexperienced mint was in trouble from the start. The volume of production was often lower than anticipated, because the mint had difficulty in attracting the amount of metal needed to keep its machinery in full production. One reason for this was the scarcity of various kinds of metals used for making coins. Native metal resources were as yet un-

*Figure 16.* (a) *Half cent, 1793.* (b) *Large cent, 1793.*
(c) *Half disme, 1792. Right:* (d) *Half dollar, 1794.*
(e) *Five-dollar gold piece, 1798.* (f) *Ten-dollar gold
piece, 1795.* (American Numismatic Society)

developed and were unable to relieve the shortage.
Had the government been able to purchase and
furnish its own supply of metal, as it later did, the
results might have been much more satisfactory.

Metal furnished for early U.S. coins came from
numerous sources. In his book *Early American
Cents,* Dr. William H. Sheldon reported that some
of the copper came from Sweden, some from England, and some was obtained by melting copper
nails, spikes, and copper finishings from wrecked
ships, including both British and American men-of-

war. Some of it came from kitchen and other house-
hold utensils donated or sold to the mint in response
to urgent appeals. George Washington is said to have
donated "an excellent copper tea-kettle as well as
two pairs of tongs early in 1793 for the first cents."
Similar contributions were made by other government officials.

Foreign coins were also a source of metal for making the new American pieces. The Bank of Maryland,
the mint's first depositor of silver, sent $80,715 in
French coins to the establishment in July 1794. The

first gold deposited at the mint, however, came from a Boston merchant in the form of ingots, in February 1795. He later received U.S. gold coins in payment.

PORTRAITS AND DESIGNS ON COINS

Although the engravers were directly responsible for the artistic designs which identify a coin, public opinion also played an important role in determining their subjects. Should the portrait of Washington or the Goddess of Liberty appear on the face of the U.S. dollar? This question aroused considerable controversy, for though the Senate strongly favored honoring the first President, the House and many other people contended that it would remind them of the king's image on English coins. The Goddess was finally chosen, and not only graced the dollar but other coins of the nation for more than a century to follow.

It may be noted that through the years the portrait of the Goddess underwent many changes. Her hairdos on early bust-type portrayals were often changed along with other details in the design of the coins. For some years after 1840 she was a seated figure. Later, on the Saint-Gaudens $20 gold piece of 1907 and on the 1916 design of the quarter, she appeared standing.

The idea of honoring highly regarded national leaders on coins, however, persisted. The first coin to bear a Presidential portrait was the cent piece issued in 1909 to mark the centennial of Lincoln's birth. Since then, Washington, Jefferson, Franklin, Franklin D. Roosevelt, and John F. Kennedy have all been honored with their portraits on coins ranging from the nickel to the half dollar. A number of other statesmen and outstanding persons have also had their portraits on various U.S. commemorative coin issues. In no case, however, has a President's image appeared on a coin until after his death. Where such portraits are used, the word LIBERTY also appears.

The first U.S. gold and silver coins to come from the mint all featured another emblem: the American eagle—a familiar figure that has since appeared on many coin issues (figure 17). This proud bird of prey was so prized by the people that the name "eagle," as has already been noted, was given to the gold pieces. The $10 gold coin was known as the eagle; the $2.50 and $5 pieces became the quarter eagle and half eagle; and the $20 gold piece, first struck in 1907, became the double eagle. The figure of the eagle, an ancient symbol, had previously appeared on certain copper coins issued by the states.

Similarly, the use on state and pattern coins of stars to represent the original thirteen states was continued in the design of the early U.S. silver and gold coins. The copper coins, too, in 1808 and 1809, adopted this emblem and continued it until 1857. As the number of states increased, it was found to be difficult to design coins with stars for more than the original thirteen states without their seeming

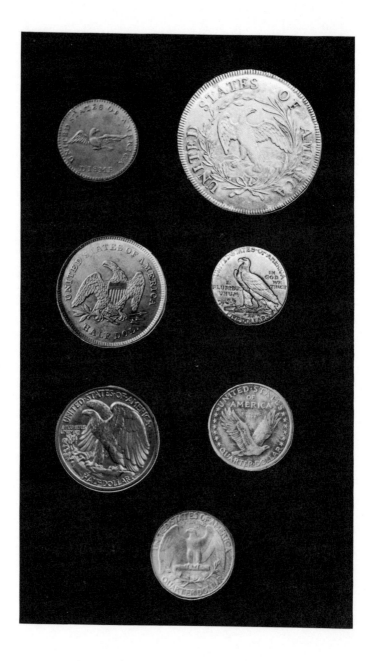

crowded. In a few instances, however, this has been achieved—for example, in two relatively recent issues. The 1907 $20 piece has forty-six stars, and the 1964 John F. Kennedy half dollar bears stars representing all fifty states.

Through the years two mottoes have appeared repeatedly on U.S. coins. The earlier of these, E PLURIBUS UNUM (One Composed of Many), appeared on the $5 half-eagle gold pieces in 1795 (figure 16). This motto, expressing unity among the states, had been previously used on a state coin, the New Jersey cent. The other familiar motto, IN GOD WE TRUST, made its debut on the bronze 2-cent piece issued in 1864 during the Civil War. It expressed a popular religious sentiment, and the motto has persisted ever since on the nation's coins.

*Figure 17. Variations in design of the American eagle. (a) Early disme. (b) 1796 dollar. (c) Half dollar, 1839. (d) Five-dollar gold piece, 1929. (e) Half dollar, 1916. (f) Quarter dollar, 1916. (g) Quarter dollar, 1932.* (American Numismatic Society)

# 9

# THE ERA OF THE
# NATIONAL BANKS

After wrestling for many generations with foreign coins and sundry monetary problems, Americans looked forward to using coins of their own. They were bitterly disappointed. The period from the opening of the mint in 1793 to about 1853 was one of the most unstable and confusing in the entire history of the country. Important improvements in the coinage system were made in the 1830's and after the gold discoveries of 1849, yet coinage remained inadequate up to the early 1850's. The output of coins was relatively small and a large number of them never got into circulation. Throughout the period, many worn, clipped, and underweight foreign coins continued to circulate, although in diminishing numbers. And because not enough coins of any kind were available, the use of paper money developed early and increased rapidly. Much of the paper money was of uncertain value. Some of it, notably the issues of inferior banks, referred to as "wildcat banks," was utterly worthless. This was also the era of fractional paper notes—called "shinplasters" or scrip—and copper tokens, all of which were circulated to create needed small change.

COINAGE REFLECTS PROBLEMS OF A NEW NATION
The currency problems merely reflected the sectional, political, and economic difficulties of a new and rapidly growing nation. When the United States began its coinage, its population was little more than 4 million, largely confined to the original thirteen states along the Atlantic seaboard. There were additional islands of population in the western territories, which were soon to become states. But what profound changes took place in sixty years! The national boundaries extended from coast to coast and the population was nearing 25 million in 1850. Whereas one mint was operating in 1793, by 1853 four were turning out millions of new gold and silver coins so long needed in the arteries of trade at home and abroad. Some landmarks of the period in between were the Louisiana Purchase (1803), which doubled the nation's land area; the acquisition of Florida (1819); and the annexation of Texas (1845). The Mexican Cession (1848) took in a vast new territory in the West that included California, a land that produced more gold than Americans had ever dreamed of.

Along the way the United States had fought two wars, the War of 1812 against England and the Mexican War, and had survived threats to national unity from the various sections. It had also survived several financial panics, including the famous one of 1837. It had passed through the era of turnpikes into the age of steam and steamboats, canals, railroads, and into the beginnings of the age of electricity. Along with scientific progress had come broad manufacturing and industrial development, particularly in New England and other parts of the North. Shipping and commerce, which had been confined largely to the northern seaport cities during the two previous centuries, continued in far greater volume and variety during the first half of the nineteenth century.

THE POLITICS OF SECTIONALISM

The growing financial power of the nation showed itself in expanded business enterprise and in banking, a new financial facility developed in the late 1700's. Both business and banking had become more and more centered in the northeastern states, particularly in the big cities of New York, Philadelphia, and Boston. This concentrated financial power was increasingly feared by southern planters, by small farmers in the back country, and also by laboring men in the big cities. The split between the business and financial interests on the one hand and the farming and working-class interests on the other took political form very early. The Federalist party, in power under Presidents Washington and John Adams, tended to speak for the financial and manufacturing groups in the Northeast. The Republican, or Anti-Federalist, party (the present day Republican party was not established until the 1850's), which came to power under Jefferson in 1801, was most influential in the rural areas of the South and West. Political differences between sections of the country continued to grow, though the parties that represented these regions changed their names.

Jefferson and Hamilton, the two men who worked so hard to establish a system of coinage, were at opposite poles politically. Jefferson, a Republican, believed that the federal government should remain small and democratic and should favor the agricultural interests. He wanted to interpret the Constitution literally, so that Congress would be unable to take over from the states more powers than the Constitutional Convention had specifically granted to it. Hamilton, a leading spokesman for the Federalist party, favored a strong, centralized federal government that would be dominated by the financial and industrial aristocracy. He preferred, therefore, to interpret the Constitution liberally. This conflict between the advocates of "states' rights" and those of a strong national government is a basic political issue in the United States even today.

HAMILTON'S ECONOMIC PROGRAM

Hamilton's economic program as Secretary of the Treasury included the establishment of a national bank. The First Bank of the United States, chartered by Congress in 1791 for a twenty-year period, was to be controlled to some extent by the government. It would have a monopoly of the government's banking business, but one-fifth of its directors would be appointed by the government. The purposes of the national bank were many. It would boost the economy by making loans to encourage business and agriculture. It would issue paper money, redeemable in coin, and would help in regulating the state-chartered banks. It would aid the government by providing a safe place to deposit federal funds and by making it easier to collect taxes. As Hamilton had predicted, the B.U.S., as it was called, did much to stabilize the national economy for many years. Hamilton did not live to see the success of his plan, for he was killed in a duel with Aaron Burr in 1804.

In spite of its usefulness, the B.U.S. had many enemies. Foremost among them was the President. Jefferson believed that the bank was unconstitutional because the Constitution did not specifically authorize the Congress to charter a bank. Although the Supreme Court decided that the bank was constitutional, many others, particularly farmers, called it "the Octopus." It was controlled by wealthy men of the industrial Northeast, whom the farmers thought were out of sympathy with the rest of the country. Smaller state-chartered banks, too, did not like it because it prevented them from lending freely or from issuing too many paper notes.

Other parts of Hamilton's economic program were

*Figure 18. The Bank of the United States branch at Wall Street (pillared building), circa 1826.* (Chase Manhattan Bank Collection, Moneys of the World)

also intended to improve economic stability and to help the growth of industry. Hamilton believed that in order to strengthen the new government the propertied classes had to be given a stake in it. He planned to fund the public debt at face value—that is, to give new interest-bearing bonds in place of the old bonds issued by the old Congress during and after the Revolution. Naturally, this proved to be profitable for holders of the old bonds, which had declined greatly in value. Next, Hamilton recommended that state debts be taken over by the government. In both cases the national debt would be increased. But Hamilton was one of the first economists to believe in a large national debt, because he felt that in this way the government's creditors would be tied to the new government. Critics of Hamilton's plan were largely Anti-Federalists who later became Jeffersonian Republicans. They argued that both funding plans would benefit speculators, who bought the securities from the original holders at a fraction of their value. Nevertheless, the program was passed. The new government was given sound financial backing and national prosperity rose.

THE NEW COINS FAIL TO CIRCULATE

The U.S. Mint at Phildelphia had inadequate machinery and its inexperienced directors often followed coinage policies that would not work. In the first seven years the mint produced less than $2 million in coins. These included about $700,000 in gold coins, principally $5 and $10 pieces; about $1.2 million in silver coins, mostly dollars and half dollars; and about $50,000 in copper pieces, chiefly cents. Even if all these coins had reached the public, they would have amounted to only a fraction of the coins in use, most of which were Spanish. But most of the U.S. coins produced before 1800 and for the next several decades never got into circulation. About 95 per cent of the entire coinage up to 1830 was in gold and large silver pieces. Many of these went into bank vaults to help secure the paper money that was gradually taking the place of coins. Vast amounts of coins, however, were looked upon merely as metal to be used or traded with. Manufacturers of gold and silver products melted down coins to obtain the metal they needed. Speculators also found that they could make a small profit by shipping the new U.S. silver dollars (later, half dollars, too) to the West Indies. There they were readily accepted and could be traded for the Spanish dollars of heavier silver content. In turn, the Spanish pieces could be brought to the U.S. Mint and profitably recoined. And again the vicious circle was continued.

As a result of these conditions the silver dollar was rarely seen in circulation, though more than 1.4 million of them were made between 1794 and the completion of the issue dated 1803. Consequently, minting of the dollar was stopped by the director of the mint, and the decision was officially confirmed by President Jefferson in 1806. At the same time coinage was stopped on the gold eagle, which also tended to disappear from circulation.

GOLD COINS UNDERVALUED

Before the turn of the century the 15 to 1 ratio of the value of gold to silver, established by Congress, was found to be out of line with the world price ratio. The ratio on the world market reached as high as 15¾ to 1 in 1799, and France adopted a ratio of 15½ to 1 in 1803. Consequently, gold coins were worth more as bullion—that is, gold bars—than as coin. They were bought and melted down as soon as they were minted and were rarely seen in circulation. This situation was to continue until 1834, when the ratio was changed to 16 to 1.

## HALF DOLLARS

Half dollars were the only coins produced in considerable volume by the mint. Of the total U.S. output of about $35 million in gold, silver, and copper pieces between 1793 and 1830, about two-thirds were half dollars. The mint was under constant criticism from members of Congress and others because of its inadequate output and relatively high costs of operation. It therefore concentrated on making half dollars in order to produce more money at less expense in a shorter time than it could if it produced smaller denominations. Another reason for the mint's decision to concentrate on producing half dollars was that they were in demand from banks. Consequently, these coins, too, were seldom seen, for they vanished into bank vaults. Many of the early half dollars that have survived to the present day are still in excellent condition because they never circulated.

## OUTPUT OF FRACTIONAL COINS

The few quarters, dimes, and half dimes produced during the period up to 1830 did manage to get into circulation. This was probably because they contained too little silver for metal speculators to bother with. But these small silver coins amounted to only 3 per cent of the value of the mint's total output during the period. In fact, less than one of these coins was minted for each person living in the United States in 1830. During nineteen of the thirty-seven years between 1793 and 1830, no quarters were minted; in thirteen of the years no dimes were made; and in twenty-six of the years no half dimes were made.

Copper coins, the cent and half cent, were also produced on a relatively small scale. Though the large cents were issued every year, the yearly output up to 1830 was less than $15,000. The half cents produced in only twenty of the years between 1793 and 1830, mostly between 1800 and 1810, were in least demand of all our coins. Apparently people did not want to bother with coins of such small value. For one thing, people in the first part of the nineteenth century did not make so many trade transactions for small profit as they do today. Moreover, goods and services were frequently marked in terms of the small coins most in use, the Spanish real and half-real. Although the cent was more popular than the half cent, even it was used mostly in areas in and about the larger population centers. Many of the cents were melted down and used in manufacturing when copper was scarce.

In its early decades the U.S. Mint could not fulfill the purposes for which it was founded. It was hampered by shortsighted laws and policies. The penny pinching of Congress forced it to operate with inadequate facilities. It was caught in the net of specu-

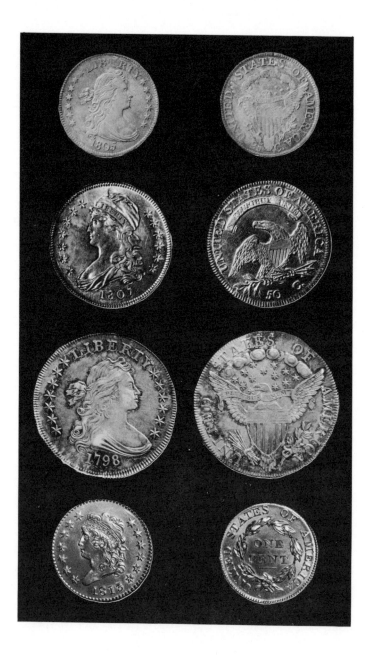

lators in money and metal. It could not, therefore, supply nearly enough U.S. coins to take the place of the foreign coins in circulation.

PAPER MONEY AND STATE BANKS

The growing new nation, however, had to have money of one kind or another, so it turned to paper money in the form of bank notes. During the relatively prosperous first decade of the nineteenth century, these notes multiplied with the rapid growth of banks, particularly those chartered by the states.

Before the Revolution there were no banks in America. If a man wanted to borrow money, he got it from an individual. But immediately after the war, banks developed as private institutions chartered by the national or a state government. Banks could not only loan money and engage in various financial services, but could also issue bank notes to be used as paper money. These notes were backed by coins and other securities deposited in the bank. Naturally the notes were only as good as the amount of coin or other security behind them. The bills of a sound bank were redeemable in coin.

The Bank of North America, established in Philadelphia in 1781, was the first bank in the United

*Figure 19. Some early mint issues. (a) Twenty-five-cent piece, 1805. (b) Fifty-cent piece, 1807. (c) One dollar, 1798. (d) One-cent piece, 1813. (Ameri-can Numismatic Society)*

States. Other important private banks were soon established in New York, Boston, and other cities. As has already been noted, the most important of all banks was the First Bank of the United States (1791–1811). The notes issued by such banks generally became good money because the banks could, if need be, redeem their bills in coin.

We have seen what happened to the "bills of credit" paper money issued by the Continental Congress and also by the states during the Revolutionary period. Most of it became worthless because it could not be redeemed at face value by the respective governments issuing it. After the federal government was established, only Congress had the power to issue money. Although the states no longer had this power, they could charter banks which could issue paper money as long as it was redeemable in coin. State-chartered and other private banks began issuing many millions of dollars in paper money. Some of this money was perfectly good. Much of it was only partly good and some of it was worthless because it lacked proper security or had no security at all.

The state-chartered banks, referred to as state banks, were by far the most numerous. In 1801 there were about thirty state banks in the country. The number grew to seventy-five in 1805 and to eighty-eight in 1811. By that date, according to Secretary of the Treasury Albert Gallatin, $28 million in bank notes had been issued by the banks. From then on the issuing of paper money ran wild and resulted in a time of financial chaos.

PERIOD OF THE WAR OF 1812

An important factor in this chaotic situation was the temporary absence of a Bank of the United States. Its charter had expired in 1811 and, because of political squabbles, it was not renewed until 1816. In the meantime, it could not exercise its stabilizing role over banking. The state banks multiplied without control during the difficult years of the War of 1812. Their number expanded to 208 by 1815, when their bank-note issues were reported as high as $100 million in face value. Their real value, however, had slumped in most cases.

In 1814, at the depth of this period of financial disorder, banks throughout the country suspended redemption of their notes in coin, and most people continued to accept the notes at a lower value. Only in New England, where state control over the banks was more effective than elsewhere, did the state bank notes continue to be accepted at face value.

An important reason for the continued use of depreciated paper money was that coins had disappeared from circulation. Even the small fractional pieces of money were temporarily gone. Municipalities, insurance companies, turnpike companies, and even business firms issued scrip, or shinplasters, which were eagerly accepted in local circulation.

Where had the coins gone? Some remained in

bank vaults to support paper money, but some had left the country. They were taken from the banks to make necessary wartime purchases overseas. Many of the coins were simply hoarded by individuals. It was another case in which bad money—the less valuable paper money—drove out good money, not only coins but also the better kinds of paper money.

THE MONEY REVOLUTION

U.S. money had been revolutionized by banking and bank-note issues. Coins had comprised most of the currency around 1800, according to Secretary of the Treasury Gallatin. By 1811 about half of all available coin had been taken over by the banks in support of their paper currency and other operations. This forced the people to become more and more dependent on paper money.

For many decades—almost until the Civil War period—the paper money situation would remain little changed. Coinage production by the United States would be notably improved from time to time, but the big paper-money mill, supported by banking and business and inept government policies, would grind on.

ERA OF READJUSTMENT AND EXPANSION

The Bank of the United States was rechartered in 1816 for another twenty-year period. It regained much of its control over the nation's banking system. Inflation and higher prices following the war were brought to a halt with the aid of the bank. But many banks failed when they were asked to redeem their bank notes, because they did not have the coin to do this. Arthur Nussbaum, in his *History of the Dollar,* writes that state-chartered bank notes, said to amount to $100 million in 1815, shrank to $49 million during the bank crisis of 1819. By the next year they fell to $41 million. On the other hand, many banks that survived the crisis improved their stability at least temporarily by adopting stricter rules in issuing bank notes.

Meanwhile, state financing, such as that of New York for building the Erie Canal (completed in 1825), and business financing, in the building of railroads and other enterprises, were rapidly taking the center of the stage once occupied by the federal government. Moreover, European capital poured into frontier land expansion, as well as other private enterprises. It was in this period of relative prosperity that Democrat Andrew Jackson became President (1829) and launched his war against the Second Bank of the United States (1816–1836).

Despite the usefulness of the bank, President Jackson, like many other Americans, feared the growing power of "the Octopus." At that time the bank had twenty-six branch offices across the country. Its president, Nicholas Biddle, wanted to curb the uncontrolled expansion of the state banks in their lending and issuing of notes. He particularly angered the South and West, where the state banks were more overextended in their loans and services than else-where. Another source of complaint against the B.U.S. was that it was controlled by wealthy men of the industrial Northeast. Their interests were felt to be in conflict with those of the primarily agricultural population of the country at large.

Thus, although Congress passed a bill for rechartering the bank in 1832, President Jackson vetoed the measure and ordered the removal of government deposits from the bank the following year. The bank's federal charter expired in 1836 and was never renewed. With the end of the bank's national influence, the country would ride unbridled on a wave of expansion and prosperity which was to come to an abrupt halt with the Panic of 1837.

# 10

# COINAGE IMPROVEMENTS INAUGURATE THE ERA OF GOLD

The American people had heard a lot of talk about gold during the nation's formative years. They knew that the coinage system fashioned by Hamilton and Jefferson was bimetallic, but they had actually seen very few gold coins up to the 1830's. Suddenly in the 1830's Americans could occasionally find gold coins in their pockets. There were two reasons for this change. First, the United States had discovered gold mines of its own. Second, it changed the coinage ratio in favor of gold.

GOLD-SILVER RATIO CHANGED

Up to 1834 our bimetallic coinage laws had rated gold fifteen times more valuable than silver. But long before this date gold began to bring higher prices in the world market. In 1799 the price reached a ratio of $15\frac{3}{4}$ to 1. This rise was reflected in the coinage systems of other countries, notably England and France. France adopted a ratio of $15\frac{1}{2}$ to 1 in 1803.

So, soon after it began, our system was out of date. Silver coins were proportionally worth more than gold. As a result, gold coins, both domestic and foreign, disappeared from circulation more quickly than silver pieces. To correct the situation, we changed the gold-silver ratio to 16 to 1 in 1834. Gold coins were called sixteen times more valuable than silver. Thus began what some have called the "golden age" of American metallic currency, even though the system continued to be bimetallic. The U.S. did not adopt a gold standard until 1873. However, the steps taken in 1834 and later, in 1853, can be considered moves in that direction. In taking the overdue corrective steps in 1834, Congress simply reduced the pure gold content of the gold dollar unit from 24.75 to 23.2 grains. The amount of pure silver in the silver dollar remained unchanged at 371¼ grains. Thus, by lessening the amount of pure gold in the gold dollar unit (no actual gold coin of that denomination existed), the new ratio of approximately 16 to 1 was achieved.

It was soon found that the new ratio was a mistake. Instead of bringing the country back to a balanced bimetallic currency, the new ratio had undervalued silver and overvalued gold. In the world market gold was valued at 15.625 to 1, and Congress had considered adopting that ratio. But political pressure, particularly from the new gold-producing regions of the South, influenced Congress to adopt the 16 to 1 ratio. And as a result gold coins began to circulate as never before.

Minor revisions in our coinage law were made in January 1837, providing a uniform fineness of .900 for both gold and silver coins. That is, nine parts of each denomination would be pure metal and the remaining part would be alloy. In this adjustment the pure gold in the gold dollar was increased by a mere .02 grain, while the standard weight (the weight of the whole coin) remained 25.8 grains. The pure silver content of 371¼ grains in the silver dollar was untouched, but the standard weight was reduced from 416 to 412½ grains. These changes made the new legal ratio of the two metals 15.998 to 1. This did not greatly improve the balance.

OUR VANISHING COINS

These changes did nothing to solve the biggest money problem that the U.S. had wrestled with since its coinage began: its gold and silver pieces had such high intrinsic value that they were primarily considered as metal, not as coin. Their pure metal content was roughly equivalent to their face value because Hamilton and those who followed him would not tolerate any kind of "debasement." Consequently, speculators could profit by trading with the coins as gold and silver. If Congress had been willing to reduce the pure metal content of silver coins, the U.S. would have created what is known as a "subsidiary" coinage. That is, these coins could not have been profitably sold by speculators and would have tended to stay in circulation. Corrective measures of this kind were finally taken in 1851 and

1853. In the latter year the pure silver content of the half dollar, quarter, dime, and half dime was reduced about 7 per cent. Two years earlier the mint had introduced the silver 3-cent piece containing less pure silver than any previous silver coins.

The silver dollar, however, retained its silver content of 371¼ grains, although in 1837 the amount of alloy in the piece was changed to make the coin 3½ grains lighter. As a result it remained a little-known coin during much of its lifetime, seldom seen in circulation until late in the 1870's. Its mintage, stopped in 1804, was resumed in 1840, but its yearly output continued to be small. Pattern or sample silver dollars designed by Christian Gobrecht were struck in 1836, 1838, and 1839.

### THE HOAX OF 1804

Don Taxay, in his book *The U.S. Mint and Coinage*, reports that in 1834 the State Department instructed mint director Samuel Moore to send gift sets with a sample of each coin in use to the King of Siam and the Sultan of Muscat. The eagle and the silver dollar had not been struck since 1804, but Moore decided to include them in the gift sets and ordered that dies bearing the date 1804 be prepared. In so doing, however, he was violating the law, for all coins were supposed to bear the year of their issuance. Moreover, no genuine 1804 dollar seems to have existed, for the pieces made that year were dated 1803. Moore, though he had good intentions, was guilty of perpetrating a hoax. Duplicate sets of the coins were ordered by the State Department in 1835, according to Taxay, who adds: "Whether additional impressions were made at that time, or by Mint employees a few years later, eight 1804 dollars struck from these antedated dies are now known." At any rate these pieces, resulting from a hoax contrived to please a few people, are today considered by collectors to be among the most valuable of American coins.

IMPROVEMENT OF MINT FACILITIES

An important provision of the 1837 law was to establish a fund of $1 million. This enabled the mint to buy metal bullion for coinage without having, as before, to depend on private owners bringing metal into the mint. The Philadelphia Mint had moved in 1833 into a new and much larger and better-equipped building, the façade of which was graced with Greek columns. Its operations were soon completely steam-powered—a vast improvement over the early horse-powered days of operation. Soon the mint also established branches elsewhere.

Southern gold interests, not content with their success in changing the gold-silver ratio to favor gold, now wanted mints in the South. Their wishes were fulfilled by an 1835 law providing for the establishment of the first three branch mints. One, at New Orleans, was equipped for both gold and silver coinage. The others, at Charlotte, North Carolina, and Dahlonega, Georgia, both near the gold fields, were for gold coinage only. Beginning operations in 1838, these branches minted coins until the Civil War began in 1861. The Charlotte and Dahlonega branches never reopened, but the New Orleans branch, one of the most important in the system, resumed operations in 1879 and continued until 1909. Its coins were distinguished by the "O" mintmark.

The improvement of mint facilities during the 1830's led to an increase in the supply of gold coins. Some of these at last found their way into circulation as well as into bank vaults and business channels. Coinage of gold was stepped up to about $3,700,000 in 1834 and to over $4,135,000 in 1836.

Silver coins, though undervalued by the 1834 metallic ratio, did not go out of circulation to any great extent until late in the 1840's. In fact, more new silver coins than ever were struck at the mints in the 1830's. There were many more new quarters, dimes, and half dimes, as well as half dollars. After the new metallic ratio was made law, many banks sold their silver reserves at a profit and replaced them with gold. But this loss of silver was more than offset by the large quantities of the metal that began to flow into the mint from reopened mines in Mexico and other Latin American countries.

THE PANIC OF 1837

In 1837, in the midst of what seemed likely to be unending prosperity, the first severe panic in the United States occurred. It lasted for about five years, if the banking crisis which followed is included. The panic was triggered by several events, including crop failures in the mid-1830's, Jackson's Specie Circular, and a financial crisis in England. But the main cause was an overexpansion of business in America, combined with the extension of loans to many persons who could not pay them and overspeculation in western lands.

President Jackson, in order to curb speculation in land, issued his Specie Circular in 1836. This decree gave notice that the government would accept only gold and silver in payment for public lands. It was primarily aimed at land speculators in the East, but its effects were widespread. Whereas paper money had previously been used in the purchase of government land, millions in hard money were now taken from state banks to pay for these purchases. A general run on the banks followed, depleting their cash reserves. Many banks were shown to be weak.

A nationwide halt to business, particularly to banking, came in May 1837. Nearly all banks suspended payments in coin, even though an estimated $149 million in their paper notes were in circulation. Many banks and businesses soon failed. There was some recovery in 1838 and 1839, but the banks developed even worse trouble in 1841. It was reported that ninety-one of them failed and about a third of the nation's banking capital was lost. Bank-note circulation dropped to about $60 million. Though some specie payments were resumed in 1842, a more thorough recovery in banking was not achieved until 1843. Banks in the cotton-producing South and in the West were among the worst sufferers during the crisis.

It was a strange sort of panic in a number of respects. It occurred while the federal government was operating on a surplus, the entire national debt having been paid off in 1835. Much hard money was owned, but because of hoarding it was kept from circulating freely. The radical reduction in the amount of paper money, caused by bank failures and retrenchment of paper issues, also caused the people to rely more heavily upon coins as the sure "store of value." But because they were loath to part with their coin, a shortage of change developed. To take the place of the cents that had become scarce, private copper tokens, known as "hard time" or "Jackson" tokens, were issued by merchants and others in many parts of the country. The pieces resembled cents and passed for that amount. They contained less copper than the U.S. cent and consequently were profitable for the manufacturer. The tokens also served as an advertising medium. The wording on them was often political in nature, and usually critical of Jackson. Shinplasters were again used in this period.

THE PROBLEM OF FOREIGN COINS

In the early 1840's more U.S. gold and silver coins were circulating than ever before, despite a slight reduction in the mint output during the panic period. Now the nation could seriously turn its attention to an old problem, that of the foreign coins in circulation. These coins were chiefly of Mexican and Spanish-American origin. They comprised about 40 per cent of all coins in use as late as 1830, according to a Senate committee report of that year. Thus, they were still a sizable element of the coins in use. Congress had repeatedly had to pass laws to keep the foreign pieces legal tender, because they were badly needed during periods of serious coin shortage. The smaller Spanish silver coins—the double-real, the real, and the half-real or medio—were especially needed for small change, while the Spanish dollar and half dollar were rarely seen, except in banks. But in the 1840's the much-used Spanish, French, and other foreign coins were so worn, clipped, and generally underweight that the banks would accept them only by weight, which was less than their face value.

Yet foreign coins kept circulating (figure 20). People tolerated them in almost any condition, as they had done for two centuries. The prices of many goods and services showed how much the people relied on Spanish money. Quotations might be in dollars and cents, but the fractional amounts represented the Spanish coins still in use. It was still common in the 1840's to see prices quoted at 6¼, 12½, 37½, and 62½ cents, as well as at 25 and 50 cents. All of these odd amounts could be readily paid in Spanish coins. As late as 1858, Horace Greeley's

*Figure 20.* (a) *French one-franc piece, Henry V, 1831.* (b) *British florin, 1849.* (c) *Eight-real piece from Argentina, 1852.* (American Numismatic Society)

*Whig Almanac* was priced at 12½ cents a copy, the amount of a real. The New York *Herald* in 1852 advertised various goods at 37½ cents and 62½ cents, corresponding to three reals and five reals.

All this greatly complicated a coinage that the decimal system had been intended to simplify. Bank notes were always in dollars and cents. Government accounts, too, were kept in terms of dollars and cents. But for a time the postal rates for certain distances were 6¼, 12½, and 18¾ cents. And there were even lingering cases where articles were still priced in shilling and pence—further proof of the difficulty of ridding a new nation of the influence of foreign coins.

REVALUATION AND RECOINING

In 1844, the U.S. Treasury adopted a policy of recoining all foreign coins received by the government. Since vast numbers of these coins were so worn as to be no longer of the required legal weight, they were only to be accepted at less than their normal values. In 1843 the New York banks had established a scale of values, accepting the Spanish double-real (25 cents), the real (12½ cents), and the medio (6¼ cents) at no higher value than 23, 10, and 5 cents, respectively. Despite public protests, the local post office adopted the same valuations. By 1848 the New York ratings had been adopted by banks and post offices throughout the country. Although this tended to reduce the number of foreign coins in circulation, many millions of reals and medios were still available. They often brought their normal or full valuation, but were frequently reduced respectively to 12 and 6 cents.

There was much public criticism of having two different methods of valuing foreign coins, one used by the government and the banks, the other by the people in ordinary transactions. Making change became an ordeal that often resulted in financial loss. For example, a person might receive a Spanish coin at a much higher valuation than he was able to get for it from the government or a bank.

Neil Carothers, in his *Fractional Money,* tells of a peculiar situation in the South and West, where people had "careless monetary habits" and seldom used the cent and half cent in making change. He cites the supposed example of a customer's purchase of a "half bit's worth of tobacco." He might pay for it with a "bit" (12½ cents), but receive only a half dime (5 cents) in change instead of a medio (6¼ cents). In that part of the country the dime and half dime were commonly accepted in change as equivalents of the real and medio, the dime being widely known as the "short bit." By this kind of shortchanging, an unscrupulous merchant could make a 25-cent profit merely by giving his customer 10 dimes instead of 10 reals ($1.25) in change.

THE CALIFORNIA GOLD STRIKE

The discovery of gold in California in 1848, with the gold rush beginning the next year, was a momentous event for U.S. coinage. It brought gold coins into use on an unprecedented scale. At the same time it threatened extinction of the supply of silver coins, which had been undervalued by the coinage laws of 1834 and 1837. Congress took corrective measures in 1851 and 1853 that reduced the metal content of silver coins and thus created a "subsidiary" silver coinage. The nation had for the first time an abundant supply of both gold and silver coins. In fact, these steps virtually placed the United States on a "gold standard," although that standard was not officially adopted until 1873.

When the big gold strike came, the United States had been minting large numbers of gold coins from metal flowing in from abroad, as well as from mines in the southern Appalachians. Gold was attracted to this country because the 16 to 1 ratio had made it worth more here than in the world market, and our favorable trade balance increased the flow. Our gold coinage (figure 21) had risen to the $8 million mark in 1843, dropped to half that in 1846, then risen to $20 million in 1847. In 1850, after the gold strike, it rose to $31 million and climbed to more than $62 million the following year. Coins included not only the eagle ($10), the half eagle ($5), and the quarter eagle ($2.50), but two new gold pieces, the $1 gold piece and the double eagle ($20). These last two were, respectively, the smallest and the largest gold coins we ever produced.

NEW GOLD COINS

As authorized by the Coinage Act of March 3, 1849, the gold dollar had a weight of 25.8 grains and was 9/10ths pure gold, or .900 in fineness. The gold dollar and the $20 gold piece authorized at the same time were of the same composition as the other gold denominations. Both were designed by James Barton Longacre, a well-known Philadelphia engraver employed by the mint (figure 22). The gold dollar

*Figure 21.* (a) *Five dollars* ("*half eagle*"), *1854.*
(b) *Ten dollars* ("*eagle*"), *1843.* (c) *Two-and-one-half dollars* ("*quarter eagle*"), *1821.* (American Numismatic Society)

was particularly desired for use as a substitute for
the silver dollar, which, though it was still produced
in small quantities, rarely got into circulation (figure
22c). The tiny dollar was produced in considerable
quantities and in the early 1850's came into wide use.

The double eagle, which went into production in
1850, was impressive in size and as an emblem of
America's newfound wealth. It was produced in vast

quantities in the next few years and constituted a large part of the total value of U.S. gold coins for a decade. It was particularly desired for use in bank reserves and for purchases abroad.

REDUCTION OF SILVER COIN SUPPLY

As gold coins began to flow from our mints in great quantities, the price of gold in the world market dropped, while the price of silver in relation to gold rose. A dollar in silver coins soon became worth as much as $1.04½. Consequently, silver coins, the better foreign pieces as well as American, began to disappear rapidly from circulation. All but the least desirable, badly worn, and clipped foreign pieces were melted down, because they were now worth more as metal than as coin.

History seemed to be repeating itself. As in the past, gold and the larger silver coins were taken from circulation because of their high intrinsic metal worth. This time, however, the 1834 and 1837 laws enacted by Congress, overvaluing gold and under-valuing silver, made matters worse. What is more, Latin America, which had been supplying the United States with much of its silver, now greatly curtailed its silver exports. Consequently, U.S. mintage of silver coins dropped considerably from the late 1840's until 1852. Something had to be done, or soon the country would have none of the silver coins so necessary to retail trade.

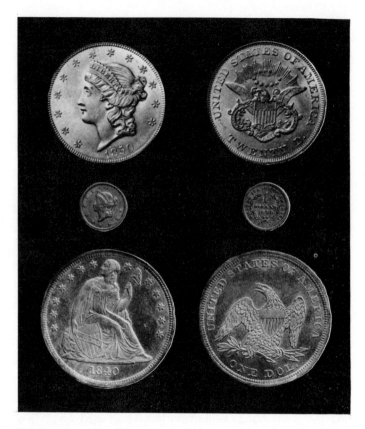

*Figure 22.* (*a*) *Twenty-dollar gold piece, 1850.* (*b*) *Gold dollar, 1849.* (*c*) *Silver dollar, 1840.* (American Numismatic Society)

THE SILVER 3-CENT PIECE

A noteworthy remedial step was taken by Congress in March 1851, when it authorized production of the now long-forgotten and tiniest of all U.S. coins, the silver 3-cent piece, weighing only 12⅜ grains. The most important fact about this coin was that it was only 3/4ths pure silver, or .750 fine, the remaining fourth being copper. Congress authorized this debasement in order to keep the coin in circulation without fear of its being melted down. At last the government had departed from the 9/10ths pure silver requirement. In doing so it had created for the first time a subsidiary or fiduciary silver coin, which could be made at a profit and had a face value somewhat higher than its metallic worth. It was made legal tender in payments only up to 30 cents. Six million 3-cent pieces were made in 1851, and 30 million more in the next two years—and they stayed in circulation.

Why did we make such a small coin at this critical time, a coin which critics reviled as a "debased" piece? At first its main purpose was to aid in the retirement of worn Spanish real and half-real pieces still being taken in at banks and government offices. It was also designed to make it easier for the public to purchase the new 3-cent postage stamp, recently reduced from 5 cents. It was thought that people would prefer the new coin for such purchases, rather than the 1-cent pieces long in public disfavor.

Officials ignored these limitations, however, and sold the new coins in lots of a hundred in return for any other U.S. gold or silver coins. They were also given out in exchange for Spanish coins at their face values of 25, 12½, and 6¼ cents, respectively, for the double-real, real, and half-real. This practice of giving people 20 per cent more than they were used to getting for the Spanish pieces was intended to speed retirement of these coins from circulation.

Unfortunately, offering the 3-cent pieces for the U.S. and Spanish silver coins took many of the other silver pieces out of circulation at a time when silver was rapidly flowing out of the country. This fact hastened a crisis in silver coinage, which is described in the next chapter.

The first steps toward the creation of a plentiful coinage had been taken. But much was still to be done.

# 11

## PREWAR COINAGE ABUNDANCE AND PROBLEMS

The decade before the Civil War saw important changes and improvements in national coinage. For the first time in American history there was an abundant supply of U.S. coins, new silver and copper ones, as well as more gold pieces. Notable among these were fractional, subsidiary silver coins, ranging from the half dime to the half dollar. These took the place of coins of the same denominations with higher silver content and stayed in circulation.

During the 1850's the large old copper cents were replaced by smaller and more attractive new copper-nickel cents. This was the U.S. cent that carried the emblem of the flying eagle. Coinage of the old copper half cents, which had never been popular, was completely abandoned. In the same decade all Spanish, Mexican, and other foreign coins were finally deprived of their legal-tender status. They had been a major element in domestic trade for nearly two and a half centuries.

Although important goals were achieved by the Coinage Acts of 1853 and 1857, Congress and those in charge of money production made some serious mistakes. Inadequacies in the new laws and in their execution resulted in overproduction of the new coins during the 1850's. The fundamental problem was that the coinage laws were too inflexible. There were no adequate provisions for redemption—that is, taking coins out of circulation when there were too many. There were also no legal ways to readjust the coinage, as, for instance, by changing the metallic makeup of coins during emergencies like the Civil War.

NATIONAL GROWTH AND SECTIONALISM

By mid-century the nation had come a long way on the road to maturity and world power. Its 23 million people—almost six times as many as in 1789—were still primarily engaged in agriculture. But the country was rapidly becoming urbanized. Manufacturing, industry, and finance were flourishing, particularly in the northern states all the way from Maine to Illinois. Railroads were being built at a feverish pace. Although in 1790 about 95 per cent of the population had been located in the Atlantic seaboard area, only 55 per cent of the people lived east of the Alleghenies in 1850. From 1830 to 1850 the population increased only 10 per cent in the Northeast, 40 per cent in the South and Southwest, and 75 per cent in the Northwest. During these twenty years some

2.5 million people came from European lands to this country.

By 1850 cotton, the nation's most important export crop, was king more than ever in the South, which depended increasingly on slave labor. Friction between the North and South had been growing for decades, made worse by the economic differences between the two sections. Contests over the status of slavery in the western states being admitted to the Union were temporarily settled by the Missouri Compromise of 1820 and the Compromise of 1850, but during the 1850's the North and South lived in a period of uneasy truce. Meanwhile, in the Far West and Rocky Mountain areas, there continued a booming production of gold and silver, from which the most important U.S. coins were made.

THE FIRST MOVE TOWARD A GOLD STANDARD

As has been noted, the Coinage Act of February 21, 1853, created new subsidiary silver coins containing 6.91 per cent less silver than the old ones of the same denominations. These new coins had arrows, one on each side of the date, to distinguish them from the old issues (figure 23). They also weighed less. A dollar's worth of the new coins, for example, four quarters or two halves, contained 345.6 grains of pure silver, compared to 371¼ grains of pure silver in the old coins. The total weight of such coins was 384 grains, or 28.5 grains less than those of previous issues. According to law, the subsidiary silver

*Figure 23. (a) Subsidiary quarter (with arrows), 1873. (b) Full-value quarter, 1853. (American Numismatic Society)*

coins were to be sold only in exchange for gold coins. This law was soon violated. Moreover, the coins were legal tender only up to $5 in a transaction. This restriction later became a source of much complaint. Finally, the new pieces were to be coined only from metal bought by the mint.

The reaction of the new 1853 subsidiary pieces proved to be a giant step toward adoption of a gold standard. At the time, however, Congress considered the move only a temporary expedient. The fact was that bimetallism and the established gold-silver ratio of 16 to 1 had become a thing of the past. Only the silver dollar was not changed by the 1853 law—

and the few dollars that were minted continued to be gobbled up by silver speculators as soon as they were struck. Making the fractional silver pieces subsidiary gave them a status subordinate or inferior to that of gold coins, and they have retained this status. Though gold coins have not been in circulation since 1933, U.S. money, which was officially placed on the gold standard in 1873, continues to be based on the nation's store of gold in well-guarded vaults at Fort Knox, Kentucky, and elsewhere. Thus, the U.S. still has a modified gold standard.

OVERPRODUCTION OF NEW SILVER COINS

The new subsidiary silver coins were struck in large quantities soon after the passage of the 1853 law. Nine million dollars' worth of them poured from the mint during that year, and another eight million dollars' worth was struck in 1854. This amounted to more than 50 million half dollars, quarters, dimes, and half dimes minted during the two years. The output of these coins continued on a relatively large scale until the Civil War, despite the fact that it was soon evident too many were being produced.

The American people, who had suffered so long with an unsatisfactory currency, now had plenty of coins for the first time in their lives. The reduction in silver content in the new coins didn't bother anyone. While the old silver coins—if any could be found in circulation—had about $1.04 worth of silver in them, the new ones contained only the equivalent of 97 cents of silver, or 6.91 per cent less. They passed, however, for the value of a dollar in gold. Fortunately, during the 1850's the value of silver in the world metal market remained fairly stable. If the price of silver had risen sharply, the new coins would have disappeared into the hands of speculators, just as earlier silver coins had done. This did actually happen when the war came.

By law the new coins were to be paid out by the mint only for gold coins. This law was almost immediately violated by mint officials, who exchanged them for silver bullion. They also used them to retire remaining foreign silver pieces. But paying $1.21 per ounce for silver practically erased the seigniorage, or profit, the government should have realized from the new coins.

By 1855 so many of the pieces had been minted that they glutted the channels of trade. Since they could not be redeemed at the mint and could not be accepted as legal tender for more than $5, they had nowhere to go. Businesses that had acquired large numbers of the coins finally had to sell them to brokers at a discount in order to get rid of their surplus. The mint itself built up a large surplus of them. A radical reduction in the minting of 3-cent silver coins and gold dollars in 1854 helped in a small way to correct the situation. Reduction in the mintage of the fractional silver pieces also helped to prevent further oversupply.

THE COPPER-NICKEL CENT OF 1857

The coinage law enacted on February 21, 1857, had two major features. It finally denied legal-tender status to foreign coins and it introduced nickel into U.S. coinage by creating the new copper-nickel cent. Both features served the purpose of retiring foreign coins in circulation. At the same time, the unpopular denomination of the half cent was abolished.

In the early 1850's the price of copper rose so far that it cost the government more to produce pure copper coins than they were worth. The cent (figure 24a), weighing 168 grains, was entirely too large and it became black and unattractive with use. The new cent (figure 24b) of 72 grains, 88 per cent copper and 12 per cent nickel, was much smaller and more attractive, featuring the flying eagle designed by James Barton Longacre. In 1859 this design was replaced by an Indian head, which continued on all mintages of the piece until 1909 (figure 24c). This piece is still familiar to most Americans. The 1857 coin was of the same diameter as the present cent but was somewhat thicker.

The mint was to use the new cents to buy not only gold, silver, and copper coins, but also Spanish and Mexican pieces at their full face value, regardless of how worn they were. The foreign coins had previously been redeemed at discounts of as much as 20 per cent below their face value. As a result three million dollars worth of them were still in circulation. Since the bargain rate was designed to

*Figure 24. (a) Pure copper large cent, 1848. (b) Copper-nickel cent, 1857. (c) Indian-head cent, 1872. (d) Three-dollar gold piece, 1854.* (American Numismatic Society)

encourage people to retire the Spanish coins quickly and finally, it was to last only for a period of two years. After that the government would accept the coins at 20 per cent less value.

Merchants, brokers, and others who were eager to take advantage of the offer flocked to the Philadelphia Mint on May 25, 1857, the day on which the new cents were issued for the first time. The Philadelphia *Bulletin* reported:

> *Every man and boy in the crowd had his package of coins with him. Some had their roleaux of Spanish Coin done up in bits of newspaper or wrapped in handkerchiefs, while others had carpet bags, baskets and other carrying contrivances, filled with coppers—"very cheap and filling," like boarding-house fare.*
>
> *The officiating priests in the temple of mammon had anticipated this grand rush, and every possible preparation was made in anticipation of it. Conspicuous among these arrangements was the erection of a neat wooden building in the yard of the mint for the special accommodation of the great crowd of money-changers.*

It was further pointed out that "those who were served, rushed into the streets with their money bags and were immediately surrounded by an outside crowd, who were willing to buy out in small lots at an advance of from thirty to a hundred per cent, and some of the outside purchasers even huckstered out the coin again in smaller lots at a still heavier advance."

Probably never in U.S. history did a new coin have such a popular reception. But in a few weeks the "copper-nicks" were plentiful at face value, and, like the subsidiary silver issues, they were soon over-supplied.

Despite the effectiveness of copper-nickel cents in getting rid of many Spanish coins and the large copper pieces, some of these remained in circulation long afterward. The two-year period for exchange of the Spanish pieces for cents was extended in 1859 for another two years, but the extension was canceled in 1860, by which time about 95 million of the new cents had been minted. In remote areas of the country the Spanish coins continued to be used, despite the fact that they were no longer legal tender. Although many of the old coppers were exchanged for new copper-nickel cents, even after 1900 some of these perfectly legal old coppers would turn up in change at country stores.

During the late 1850's, as the vast majority of foreign coins were being eliminated from circulation for good, price quotations and reckoning in terms of Spanish and English money disappeared from newspapers and other publications. From then on the reckoning of money in terms of the decimal system of dollars and cents became the "popular as well as official" method, according to a historian of the period.

In its smaller and more convenient and attractive form, the cent after 1857 became more useful than ever, particularly in the populated East. The coin was soon overproduced, however, because of its purpose of retiring foreign coins. It was reported that in 1860 business establishments receiving large numbers of cents were obliged to dispose of them at a discount, suffering financial losses.

GOLD COINS

Important as the silver and cent pieces were in everyday business dealings, gold represented the major element in the value of hard money being created at the mints. From 1850 to 1860 gold coinage amounted to about $373 million, and some $300 million of this amount was in $20 gold pieces alone. The total value of the gold coins struck was nearly seven and a half times more than the $47 million in silver pieces, plus the little more than $1 million in cents coined during the decade. Naturally, the people saw only a small per cent of the gold in circulation, as most of it went into bank reserves or was shipped abroad in settlement of adverse balance in international payments.

A new gold unit, the $3 piece, appeared in 1854 (figure 24d), but because little need was found for this denomination, its mintage was small, and it was discontinued in 1889. Private gold pieces were also issued from the gold-mining areas, first in Georgia and North Carolina from about 1830 to the early 1850's, and then in California from 1849 to 1855 in considerable amounts. The denominations ranged from 25-cent octagonal pieces, struck in California from 1852 to 1882, to $50 pieces. Moffat & Company of San Francisco was one of the largest producers. Although many of the pieces closely resembled U.S. coins, their private source was indicated. Mormon gold pieces were also struck in Utah, and other pieces were issued by firms in Colorado. In 1882 the United States passed a law forbidding private coinage. Before the U.S. branch mint was established in San Francisco in 1852, however, private gold was a much used form of money in the West. In most cases, too, it was of excellent quality.

BANKING IMPROVEMENTS

The 1850's saw a vast coinage of gold and improvements in silver and other fractional pieces of money. Nevertheless, until the Civil War, most money continued to be paper issues of banks established under state law. In 1860 the 31.5 million people in the country had an estimated $332 million in circulation—$207 million in bank notes and $125 million in coin. The total amount of coins in the country had grown from $96 million in 1845 to $235 million in 1860. Of this, about $110 million was in bank reserves or otherwise not circulating. And during this fifteen-year period circulation of bank notes more than doubled, rising from $90 million in 1845 to $207 million in 1860.

Banks and the quality of their paper money had

greatly improved in the years from 1845 to 1860, at which time there were about sixteen hundred of them in the country. New York City, with a population of 1.2 million in 1860, had become the financial capital of the nation. It was a leader in the movement for banking reform and in strengthening the value of paper currency by requiring that this currency be supported by adequate reserves of coin and other securities. Several states adopted strict regulations and thereby improved the paper issues of their banks.

THE UNITED STATES ENTERS BANKING

An important development in the period from 1840 to 1860 was the creation of the "Independent Treasury" system, whereby the federal government became its own banker. This system, intended to discourage speculation and protect government funds, was established under President Martin Van Buren in 1840. It provided that government funds, revenues, and receipts from land sales would be taken from private banks and placed in various sub-treasuries throughout the country. The extent to which government money previously going into the banks now went into the sub-treasuries is shown by the fact that by 1855 the new institutions held about half as much gold as did all the thirteen hundred banks in existence at that time.

The government was soon to produce its own

paper money, too, including the famous "green-backs," and was generally to strengthen its control over all forms of money. The Independent Treasury system continued to function until it was replaced by the Federal Reserve System in the twentieth century.

# 12

# THE EFFECTS OF
# THE CIVIL WAR
# ON OUR MONEY

The nation's currency was significantly influenced by the Civil War. As they had during the Revolution, coins tended to go out of circulation in all sections of the country except the Pacific Coast. A variety of coin substitutes and paper money took over. In the North, the war brought vast changes in the kinds of money that the federal government and other sources made available. In the South, the war brought monetary chaos. One of the most important results of the conflict, however, was that it led to a complete nationalization of U.S. currency. Paper, as well as coin, issues were thereafter backed by the federal government.

MAJOR CHANGES IN THE NORTH
When the war began on April 12, 1861, with the bombardment of Fort Sumter by the Confederates, there was an abundant supply of both gold and subsidiary silver coins in circulation in the North.

*151*

Very soon, however, gold and then silver pieces vanished from circulation as paper money, issued in large quantities to finance the war, depreciated in value. Few, if any, of the gold and silver coins were to be found in the channels of trade after the summer of 1862. Copper-nickel cents and new 2-cent bronze coins, which appeared in 1864, were struck in large quantities and did circulate to fill a small part of the void. But so considerable was the loss of gold and silver coins that even stepped-up production of minor coins was inadequate to meet small-change needs.

In the wartime emergency a number of different coin substitutes were used, such as ordinary postage stamps, shinplasters, and metallic tokens issued by merchants and others. Gradually federal government issues of fractional currency notes became the mainstay in small transactions while "United States notes," commonly referred to as "greenbacks," served for larger business transactions during the war and for many years thereafter.

CONFEDERATE MONEY

Though the southern states had a considerable amount of silver and gold coins at the start of the conflict, these coins soon disappeared into banks or elsewhere to be used in the war effort. During the war the South produced practically no coins of its own, only a few pattern pieces. A notable pattern piece was that of the United States half dollar produced at the New Orleans Mint. After the mint had been taken over by the South, a design of the Confederacy was placed on the reverse of the coin. Although later restrikes were made from the dies, only four original pieces are known to exist today.

Because the South lacked metal for coinage, it relied almost entirely on "treasury notes" (figure 25). The Confederate government and states issued them in such great quantities that, like the "Continentals" of the Revolutionary period, they became worthless before the end of the war. Notes of banks, municipalities, and private concerns were also issued in great numbers and added to the chaotic state of the currency. Shinplasters were said to have been issued to an even greater extent than in the North, and postage stamps also served as money.

AVAILABILITY OF COINS DIFFERED BY SECTION

The situation on the Pacific Coast was unique. In California and Oregon, for example, gold and silver coins, which continued to be made at the San Francisco Mint, circulated throughout the war. Consequently, in the Far West the dollar did not depreciate, as did greenbacks in the North or Confederate money in the South. In fact, the people in the Pacific states, having plenty of hard money, refused to use paper money, including greenbacks, and business was affected far less than it was in the rest of the country. Since there were no railroads to link the East to the Pacific Coast and since the federal govern-

*Figure 25. An example of Confederate money.* (Chase Manhattan Bank Collection, Moneys of the World)

ment was busy with the war, little or nothing was done during the conflict about the refusal of Westerners to accept the "lawful" paper money of the Union. Later, however, lawsuits did develop over this matter.

The country's coin holdings were preponderantly in the North at the start of the war, according to estimates by the director of the mint made in October 1861. Of the nation's coin total of from $275 million to $300 million in gold, subsidiary silver, and minor coins, the South held only some $20 million in gold coins and about $18 million in subsidiary silver coins. All the rest were in the North and West. The northern states had about $27 million in subsidiary silver coins, which were of primary use in retail trade. It also held about $20 million in state bank notes and about $1 million in cents and other minor pieces.

## THE DEPRECIATION OF PAPER MONEY
## DRIVES OUT GOLD

In spite of this abundance of coins in the North, practically all but the cents had disappeared from circulation within about fifteen months after war broke out. The reasons for this vanishing act were much the same as those which had brought about the loss of hard money during the Revolution. Essentially it was another case of coins being driven out of circulation by less valuable kinds of currency, primarily paper money. As in the past, speculation in metal played a big role. In the Civil War period, however, the paper money issued by the federal government always had substantial value, unlike the Continental bills of the Revolution and the treasury notes of the Confederacy, both of which became worthless.

When the North realized that it would have to raise considerable sums of money to finance the war, the Treasury immediately resorted to borrowing, since taxation was unpopular. An early war-financing step was the printing in 1861 of $30 million in so-called "demand notes," which gave the bearer the right "on demand" to have them redeemed in coin. They began circulation as currency, though they were not issued for that purpose and were not legal tender. They were made legal tender for two months in 1862 before being withdrawn and replaced by greenbacks in May. This move was forced by the coin shortage at that time. In the last days of their brief existence, the demand notes, no longer redeemable in coin, sold at a discount.

State bank notes, long a major form of paper currency, also had been circulating at face value, redeemable in coin. In 1862 the developing coin shortage made redemption impossible. They then sold at a discount and soon became a diminishing currency. Gradually they were replaced by the greenbacks and new national bank notes issued by banks created by the National Bank Act of February 25, 1863. Many state banks thereafter became national banks. With a 10 per cent "death tax" imposed by Congress upon state bank notes in 1865, they disappeared from circulation quite rapidly.

Many banks in the North began suspending payments in gold on paper issued in December 1861. This step immediately served to depreciate further the value of the paper money. From then on during the war years, except on the West Coast, gold was no longer considered as money, but rather as a commodity. It remained quarantined in bank reserves and private hoards or was used in payments abroad for needed supplies and maintenance of credit.

GREENBACKS

Early in 1862 hoarding gathered such momentum that the federal government took immediate steps to replace the great loss of gold by issuing a new type of paper money. The Legal Tender Act passed by Congress on February 25, 1862, authorized the first issue of "United States notes," called "greenbacks" or "legal tenders" (figure 26). It was a bold new step for the government, which had previously shied away from issuing paper money. Only in a few cases had the Treasury provided limited short-term issues of demand notes, not intended to circulate like other paper money. The paper money field had been left to banks.

The first greenback issue of $150 million was in $5, $10, $20, $50, $100, and higher denominations. Later $1 and $2 notes were added. Before the war's end a total of $450 million was issued, the value of which often reflected the failures and successes of the Union forces in waging the war. Greenbacks became the principal "lawful money" of the North. It was legal in all transactions, private or public, except for custom duties and payments of interest on government bonds, both of which required the use of gold. The greenbacks were not based on coin or other securities, but solely on the ability of the United States to make them good.

The greenbacks began to depreciate as soon as they were issued. Their value was to sink to about 75 cents per dollar before the end of 1862. It fell to its lowest point of 35 cents per dollar in 1864, when the public thought that a government move to curb speculation in gold meant that it could no longer support its paper money. In the spring of 1865, as the Union forces seemed more certain of winning the war, the value of the paper currency rose again

*Figure 26. A legal-tender ("greenback") note.* (Chase Manhattan Bank Collection, Moneys of the World)

to the 75-cent level. But it was not until fourteen years after the war that greenbacks were again accepted at face value.

The depreciation of the value of greenbacks is said to have introduced to the language the term "inflation," now in worldwide use. The word refers to the rise in prices that occurs when the public has a great deal of money, but the supply of goods is short. At such times the value of paper money is often reduced. The word "inflation" first appeared in a pamphlet, entitled "A Warning to the People: The Paper Bubble," issued by Alexander Del Mar in New York in 1864. This pamphlet bore a picture of a puffed-up balloon on its cover. The balloon represented the "relative inflation" of labor, real estate, merchandise, and other items in terms of the paper dollar.

DISAPPEARANCE OF SILVER COINS

Subsidiary silver coins in the North remained in circulation after the disappearance of gold coins, and for a time even after the greenbacks were issued. The intrinsic value of a dollar's worth of the silver coins was 97 cents in gold. They were used as long as the value of the paper dollar was at about the same level. But when the greenback value fell to around 95 cents, hoarding and speculation in silver coins began. Eventually unscrupulous speculators shipped nearly all of them to Canada and Latin American countries, where they were welcome. Several factors made this solution mutually agreeable. Canada had adopted a gold-based decimal system of coinage much like that in the U.S. in 1858, and the Canadian dollar and its units were worth about the same as those of this country. Similarly, since U.S. coin units had been largely based on the Spanish, many Latin American countries in need of more coins found that American silver pieces supplied their needs.

For several years before the war some U.S. coins had gone to Canada. But in 1862, when heavy speculation began in metallic money, the flow of subsidiary silver coins to Canada increased considerably. A broker in New York, for example, would buy up quantities of silver coins, offering a premium in paper money to get them. These coins were taken to Canada, where they were accepted as the equivalent of gold. The broker brought back the gold to the United States and sold it at a large profit for more paper money. And so the round of profiteering continued, with shipments first to Canada and later to Latin America. Very soon the North suffered the complete disappearance of its silver coins, about $25 million of them. Most of these coins left the country during the latter part of June and the first half of July 1862.

PARALYSIS OF BUSINESS

The rapid disappearance of silver coins had a paralyzing effect on retail trade. In New York City, railroads, other transportation companies, and restaurants were among those businesses which suffered most. Thousands of persons had to walk to and from their work because they lacked the coins for transportation. Early in July large premiums were offered by transportation and other concerns for the coins they needed to make change. But, in some cases, after a business acquired coins, it refused to hand them out in change. Instead, it sold the pieces to brokers for a profit.

Though many proposals were offered for solving the problem, few were worth considering. Among the best was that of Horace Greeley, editor of the New York *Tribune*. He suggested that the public should agree throughout the country to accept the half dime (5-cent piece) as worth 6 cents, the dime as 12 cents, the quarter as 30 cents, and the half dollar as 60 cents. Once the value of greenbacks fell below the level of 80 cents per dollar, still higher ratings for the silver coins would have been necessary to keep them in circulation. Greeley's proposal was ridiculed by some and was never adopted.

An efficient and practical plan, one historian has pointed out, would have been to reduce the proportion of silver to copper in the subsidiary silver coins, without making any other change. Thus, the U.S. Mint, then temporarily idle, might have been employed in making coins that would have stayed in circulation because their metallic value would have been at least as low as the value of the greenbacks.

There were many millions of cents in circulation and some 3-cent pieces too, but these coins were by no means adequate to replace the silver coins of larger denomination. Later the 3-cent silver coins also disappeared.

MONEY SUBSTITUTES

People and businesses began to find substitutes for the missing silver coins. At first $1 and $2 bank notes were cut into fractional parts, as they had been in 1837 and 1853. Many cities issued fractional notes, and soon people began to use ordinary postage stamps for money. The use of stamps became more widespread after the Secretary of the Treasury, late in July 1862, decided to legalize stamps for use as currency. This step greatly distressed the postal authorities, for their organization was in no way geared to meet the demand. Stamps, according to the secretary's plan, were made legal tender in payments to the government up to $5. A more impractical currency could not be imagined. The stamps stuck to everything they came in contact with and were soon barely recognizable. For a time some of the stamps were encased in mica, with a protective metal rim. A few of these have survived to become choice collectors' items.

In addition to cities and local governments, many private businesses and some unscrupulous individuals were active in issuing fractional notes. Many of the notes of reputable businesses served very well for a time, but those of certain concerns resulted in swindling millions of people. A large number of these shinplasters circulated freely during the end of 1862 and into 1863.

U.S. FRACTIONAL PAPER MONEY

Seeking a substitute for stamps, the Secretary of the Treasury arranged for the issuance of fractional notes called "postage currency" in denominations of 5, 10, 25, and 50 cents. They were printed, like stamps, in large sheets comprising many notes of a particular denomination. These sheets were often cut into blocks to provide $1 or other amounts for convenience in trade.

The production of these fractional notes, which began in August 1862, was at first so small that it brought little relief. Only about $7 million was printed in 1862. As the output was greatly increased early in 1863, the other private and less desirable forms of currency began to pass at discounts and gradually disappear. Late in January, for example, the New York *Herald* announced that it would no longer accept subscription payments in shinplasters. In March the Philadelphia *Ledger* reported that the city was "tolerably well supplied" with the U.S. fractional notes.

A more complete commitment of the government to this type of paper money (figure 27) came with the authorization on March 3, 1863, of a new issue of notes called "fractional currency." Production began the following October. Very similar to the postage currency, the new notes were to be sold as small greenbacks. They could be used to buy postage and revenue stamps and were redeemable under such conditions as the Secretary of the Treasury might prescribe. The Treasury itself, instead of private concerns, was to print the notes. Stronger paper and more attractive designs were used in this issue. A new 3-cent denomination was included, but, although it was useful in purchasing 3-cent postage stamps, it was largely unpopular. The little paper notes of the Civil War period and later have since become favorite items for collectors.

The fractional notes of the two series were wisely and effectively used in the northern states during the war. It has been estimated that in June 1863 about $20 million of the original postage currency notes were circulating. The fractional currency notes were intended to replace gradually the postage currency

*Figure 27. (a, b) Early examples of postage currency, redeemable directly in stamps. Right: (c) Fractional currency notes, which had limited value as legal tender.* (American Numismatic Society; Chase Manhattan Bank Collection, Moneys of the World)

notes. The amount of the latter in circulation did diminish, though at the end of the war nearly $10 million of them were still circulating. At that time more than $15 million of the fractional currency notes were also in circulation, totaling $25 million of both kinds of notes in use. This amount almost

approximated the value of the lost subsidiary silver coins in the North.

Unfortunately the little notes were extremely perishable. Millions of them were lost—destroyed in fires or otherwise—in the course of normal use during the war. J. J. Knox, in his *United States Notes* (1865), made this observation concerning the fractional notes:

> *The little notes were stuffed into the trouser pockets of the soldiers, with jackknife, the cartridge, the plug of tobacco, and other handy articles, and soon became unfit*

*for circulation. They wore out rapidly and became ragged and filthy, and were frequently returned for redemption.*

EMERGENCY ROLE OF CENTS AND TOKENS

When silver coins disappeared from the pockets of people in the northern states in July 1862, much of the burden of making small change fell immediately upon the copper-nickel cents (figure 24). Of the more than 100 million of these in circulation only 15 million to 20 million of them were in the southern states. The cents, having a metal value of only about half of their face value, stayed in circulation. To take the place of the missing quarters, half dollars, and dollars, they were often tied up in bundles of 25, 50, and 100 and were widely used that way in trade. Bus companies, theaters, and restaurants all accepted these bundles. It was reported that a New York store received so many that the floor of the room where they were deposited collapsed.

The U.S. Mint at Philadelphia stepped up its production of cents. Some 50 million were struck in 1863 and more than that amount were made in 1864. Nearly 40 million of these were new bronze cents, composed of 95 per cent copper and 5 per cent tin and zinc. This cent bore the design of an Indian head. It was thinner than the older cents. At 48 grains, instead of 72, it had the same weight as today's cent. A few of the 1864 bronze pieces bear the letter "L," the initial of the engraver, Longacre, on the ribbon of the Indian head.

Demand for the cents continued to grow to such an extent that, despite their increased production, businesses began to pay a premium for them. As in the case of the 1837 "Hard Times" tokens, Civil War cent tokens were produced in great numbers and varieties by merchants and other private sources to meet the great demand for metallic change. It has been estimated that some ten thousand varieties, totaling 50 million, of these cent-sized tokens were produced. Most of the pieces, of varied composition and design, bear the 1863 date. Although many were redeemable at the stores which issued them, millions of them were made only for profit, with no redemption possible. Use of the Indian-head design and other imitations of U.S. cents was common until they were prohibited by law in April 1864. Civil War tokens are still sought by many collectors.

NEW UNITED STATES MINOR COIN ISSUES

Tokens started to disappear from circulation in 1864, as the mint turned out more of the bronze cents and another new small-change coin, the bronze 2-cent piece (figure 28a). This coin, authorized in April of that year, weighed 96 grains, exactly twice as much as the bronze cent, and had the same metallic composition. The piece, made legal tender in amounts up to 20 cents, proved popular during the war period. About 27 million of them were struck in the first complete year of issue. Later, however, the denomination was considered to be unnecessary. Its production was discontinued in 1873. This 2-cent

*Figure 28.* (a) *Bronze two-cent piece, 1864.* (b) *Copper-nickel five-cent piece.* (American Numismatic Society)

piece is noteworthy as the first U.S. coin to bear the motto IN GOD WE TRUST. This motto had its origin in a wartime desire to express religious sentiment on U.S. coins. It thereafter adorned many of them, and its future use was established by Congress on July 11, 1955.

A 3-cent nickel coin was authorized on March 3, 1865. It was composed of 75 per cent copper and 25 per cent nickel and weighed 30 grains. This piece was considered by many to be unnecessary, since there was already a 3-cent silver piece. It was promoted, however, by the so-called "nickel interests," which argued for it as a substitute for the unpopular 3-cent paper note. The combination of copper and nickel produced an attractive coin that wore well. As a result it later found a use in the coinages of many nations. Mintage of the 3-cent piece was abandoned in 1889.

A far more popular copper-nickel coin was the 5-cent piece (figure 28b) authorized by Congress on May 16, 1866, little more than a year after General Robert E. Lee surrendered to General Ulysses S. Grant at Appomattox. This coin had the same metallic composition as the 3-cent nickel. Its fractional weight was 77.16 grains, to make it conform to a metric-weight standard then thought to be of important use in future coinage. The "nickel," as it is called today, was made redeemable in "lawful money" when presented in lots of $100. This was the first time in U.S. history that a subsidiary coin was made redeemable while still in circulation.

The new coins, 90 million of which were struck in the first four years of mintage, soon displaced many of the 5-cent paper notes and a much greater number of smaller denomination coins then in circulation, tending to make them superfluous. An oversupply of the 1-cent, 2-cent, and 3-cent pieces became a serious problem, largely because there were no adequate provisions in the law at that time for redeeming them.

VARIETY OF UNITED STATES COINS

By 1866 the American people had become accustomed to having a wide variety of coins. Seventeen different denominations with twenty-one different metallic compositions had come from the U.S. Mint since 1793. The larger gold and silver pieces were no longer seen in circulation. Nevertheless, it was possible in 1866 for a person to have in his pocket all of the following coins: six denominations in gold, ranging from the $1 to the $20 piece; six silver coins, ranging from the 3-cent silver piece to the silver dollar; the 3- and 5-cent nickel coins; the 2-cent bronze piece; a 1-cent piece each in copper, copper-nickel, and bronze; and the half cent in copper. Today we get along very well with only five coin denominations: the half dollar, quarter, dime, nickel, and cent. It is not difficult to imagine, however, how complicated money transactions must have been a century ago, when so many kinds of coins and fractional paper money had to be reckoned with.

After 1866 only two more new denominations were to be issued in U.S. coinage. These were the 20-cent silver piece, which appeared in 1875, and the $4 (Stella) pattern gold coin, issued in 1879. Although the "trade" dollar appeared in 1873, it was just another kind of silver dollar, with more silver in it, to be used for purposes of trade. Through the years the government has found that too many different coins lead to confusion and inefficiency in retail trade. So, in the natural process of usage and selection, it may be presumed that the five coins in American pockets today represent the survival of the fittest.

# 13

## SILVER'S CHALLENGE TO THE GOLD STANDARD

In the thirty-five years from the end of the Civil War to 1900 the United States was crippled by war, politically divided over economic matters, and burdened by corruption in government. Nevertheless, the nation was on the threshold of becoming a world power. It was a period of tremendous growth and expansion in which a great Industrial Revolution transformed the occupations and outlooks of millions of people. Railroads spanned the continent and crisscrossed the plains and mountains. They helped to tame the "Wild West" and to bring the products of farms and mines to the rest of the country. Oil, coal, iron and steel, and the related industries developed into big businesses. Employing large segments of the population, they played a part in creating new and larger cities. In the ranks of laborers in factories and on farms were millions of immigrants newly arrived from European lands. The population of the country more than doubled in the thirty-five-year period, approaching 76 million by 1900.

Industrial growth brought problems as well as prosperity. Until America learned how to control its industrial revolution for the betterment of all, certain segments of the population—small farmers, small-business men, and laborers in the cities—did not get their fair share of the nation's newfound wealth. This fact was pointed out by the Populists and Progressives during the period and was portrayed vividly in Henry George's book, *Progress and Poverty.* The so-called Robber Barons created industries on an unprecedented scale and helped the country become a great industrial power. But it was several decades before America instituted the political, economic, and social reforms needed to justify these industrial advances within the framework of a truly democratic society.

These problems manifested themselves in financial troubles. An overexpansion of railroad building helped to bring on the Panic of 1873. The metallic currency balance was upset by a record output of silver from western mines, making the value of silver cheaper in terms of gold. Excess mintage of silver dollars redeemable in gold, made largely to appease the "silver interests" and their allies, caused a dangerous drain on the Treasury's gold supply and led to the Panic of 1893. Meanwhile, growing labor forces in new factories increased their organization and demands, ushering in a period of tense labor-managements conflicts.

Despite increased prosperity and opportunities, there was throughout the period a tendency toward "deflation." Inflation during the war years was followed by an economic recession and lower prices, which some people blamed on a scarcity of currency. Consequently, the years between 1865 and 1900 were frequently marked by bitter political conflicts over currency matters, which tended to overshadow other issues. Even the bitter political struggle over Reconstruction of the war-torn southern states was soon replaced in national politics by financial issues. Different sections and classes wanted to use different kinds of money in solving their particular economic problems. Currency matters readily became vote-getting tools in the hands of politicians.

These conflicts generally developed between those who wanted an inflated currency, or "soft" money (some called it "cheap" money), and those who wanted a deflated currency, or "hard" money, based on a gold standard. In many respects it came to be a sectional and class struggle between farmers of the West and South, joined by laborers in the big cities, and the powerful industrial and financial interests in the North and East. This struggle resembled the conflicts between Jeffersonians and Hamiltonians during the early years of the Republic and between Jacksonians and anti-Jacksonians during the 1830's.

Most of those who favored soft money were Democrats. The powerful silver-mining interests in the West soon became aligned with the Democrats, who were persuaded to call for "free silver"—that is, free coinage of silver—which would increase silver coinage, use up the growing silver surplus, and keep its price from falling. With inflation and a more plentiful supply of money, farmers, for example, who bought in a protected market and sold their goods in an "open" or world market, felt they could get higher prices for their products and pay off their debts more easily. They ignored the fact that a plentiful supply of cheap silver would drive gold out of circulation and eventually cause U.S. currency to be worth less in the eyes of the rest of the world.

On the other hand, the advocates of hard money, who wanted a dollar worth 100 cents in gold, were generally found in the ranks of the Republican party. They felt that inflation would be a disaster for themselves and for the country as a whole. However, voters crossed party lines in many sections, and many compromises were made in the currency laws enacted by Congress. The gold standard had been definitely adopted by a Republican-controlled Congress in 1873. This standard was maintained against strong opposition during the remainder of the postwar period. Silverites called "demonetization"—that is, the discontinuation—of the silver dollar the "crime of '73" in their political campaigns from the mid-1870's onward. They won a partial victory in 1878 when coinage of silver dollars was resumed. But in the 1890's President Grover Cleveland, a Democrat, curbed the silver-dollar drain on gold and held firmly to the gold standard.

### GREENBACKS

Greenbacks, the principal form of U.S. currency during the Civil War, continued to be used, though their value fluctuated widely. Surprisingly enough, they regained a value equal to their denominations in gold on January 1, 1879. At that time the Resumption Act went into effect, permitting paper money to be redeemed in gold.

Since the late 1860's, bitter political campaigns had been waged between inflationists and anti-inflationists over the greenbacks. The latter were primarily in the ranks of the Republican party, which was in power most of the time during the terms of Presidents Andrew Johnson, Ulysses S. Grant, and Rutherford B. Hayes. They wanted to reduce the amount of greenbacks in circulation to help make them equal to gold in value. A reduction of about $44 million in the paper currency resulted soon after the war. The inflationists, on the other hand, were largely Democrats. They were later joined by "Greenbackers," who in the mid-1870's formed a separate party of their own. They blamed the postwar slump in agricultural prices on the reduction in the supply of greenbacks. They wanted to circulate more greenbacks in order to improve prices. Withdrawal of the paper currency was halted in 1868, and by 1873 $26 million of the withdrawn money was reissued. Finally, in 1878, the total of greenbacks in circulation was stabilized at $346,681,000, and thereafter was held to that amount. As the postwar recession ended, the conflict over paper currency gradually came to an end. But a bigger conflict was developing over silver and bimetallism.

THE COINAGE ACT OF 1873

An important event setting the stage for the "war over metals" had been the Coinage Act of February 12, 1873. This act is largely remembered for dropping the standard silver dollar from U.S. coinage, thereby placing the country on a gold standard. The act also generally revised the coinage laws. It eliminated from further coinage the silver 3-cent piece, the half dime, and the 2-cent piece, which by then were little used. The weight of the half dollar (though silver coins were not then in circulation) was increased slightly from 192 grains to 192.9 grains, and the quarter and dime were accordingly increased in weight to make them conform to the metric system. To indicate these weight changes, for a period of two years arrows were placed at either side of the dates on these pieces. The same step had been taken in 1853 to show that the silver content had been reduced.

The Coinage Act of 1873 also reorganized the U.S. Mint into its present form. The Bureau of the

Mint in the Treasury Department was established, with the bureau and its head, the director of the mint, located in Washington, D.C. All other mints thereafter operated as units within the bureau.

While dropping the standard dollar, the Coinage Act of 1873 also created a new kind of silver dollar, the "trade" dollar (figure 29b). It was so named because it was supposedly designed to compete with the Mexican peso (a dollar-size coin) in commerce with the Orient. The trade dollar had more silver in it than did the standard silver dollar. It weighed 420 grains, 3/4ths of a grain more than the Mexican coin, whereas the standard silver dollar weighed only 412½ grains. The primary purpose of the new coin was actually to make greater use of the growing supply of domestic silver. Though not originally intended for circulation in the United States, the trade dollar was permitted to circulate on a limited legal-tender basis. Even after its legal-tender status was repealed in 1876, the trade dollar continued to be used in many parts of the country, as well as in Oriental trade. Nearly 36 million of the coins had been struck when their mintage was discontinued in 1885. Most of them had been struck between 1874 and 1879, largely at the San Francisco Mint. This was more than four times the number of standard silver dollars made between 1794 and 1873.

The standard silver dollar had been the only silver coin not reduced in silver content in 1853, when all other silver pieces were reduced to subsidiary

*Figure 29. (a) Silver twenty-cent piece, 1876. (b) "Trade" dollar, 1873.* (American Numismatic Society)

status. Therefore, except for the standard silver dollar, the U.S. had effectively adopted the gold standard in 1853, although few people seemed to realize it at the time.

THE "CRIME OF '73"

Elimination of the standard silver dollar therefore meant elimination of the only coin that still conformed to the 16 to 1 gold-silver ratio adopted in 1837. It meant complete abandonment of the ratio and full-fledged adoption of the gold standard. Relatively few standard silver dollars, however, were minted up to 1873, and nearly all of these had disappeared into the hands of metal speculators. Therefore, the act of dropping the big coin from the mintage list attracted little immediate attention.

But around 1876, when the trade dollar lost its legal-tender status, the silver interests and the Silverites suddenly began to raise a hue and cry in Congress about the "crime of '73." They demanded that mintage of the standard silver dollar be resumed. Up to that time little had been said or done about returning to the old bimetallic system or about the future of silver coinage. But from then on a movement for free and unlimited coinage of silver was sponsored by the Democrats and also by some Republicans in the silver areas. Like the campaign for more greenbacks, the "free silver" movement was directed against maintaining the gold standard.

RETURN OF SILVER

Several major developments turned public attention to silver. Foremost was the greatly increased production of the metal and the consequent drop in price from about 1873 onward. Just as the California gold strike of 1849 had made gold plentiful and caused its price to drop, the huge silver output of the Comstock Lode and other western mines after the late 1850's caused the downward trend in silver prices. This trend was strengthened by another development, the adoption of the gold standard by Germany and other European countries.

By the mid-1870's U.S. silver could no longer be profitably exported to other countries. In fact, silver coins began to flow back into the United States. This reverse flow in the winter of 1877 included millions of the subsidiary silver coins that had been exported to Canada and Latin America during the 1862 currency crisis.

Although limited gold and silver coin production had continued after 1862, domestic circulation of these coins was confined to the West Coast. Most of the coins, until the early 1870's, had been produced at the San Francisco Mint, though the West Coast already had more of the coins than it could use. Meanwhile, in the North and East the currency had consisted of greenbacks, millions of fractional notes, national bank notes, and a large volume of such minor coins as the 5-cent nickel and lower denominations. Yet the Philadelphia Mint had continued limited production of gold and silver, as well as minor coins all during the war years and after. In fact, the mint had stepped up its output of coins about 1870, five years before silver coins began to circulate again in the North and East. Nearly all of the gold and silver coins produced at the mints from 1862 to that time were exported. These coins were, therefore, of little use to the public. They had become primarily a source of profit for the mines that furnished the metal and the speculators who exported them.

REDEMPTION OF MINOR COINS AND
FRACTIONAL NOTES

After the war the means for making change included an oversupply of minor coins and a large assortment of fractional paper notes. The small denomination coins, ranging from the cent to the 5-cent nickel, were so numerous that, as has been noted, they clogged the channels of trade. There was an urgent need for methods of redeeming these coins in order to get them out of circulation. Such a measure was finally passed by Congress on March 3, 1871. In several months millions of minor coins were redeemed with greenbacks. By 1872 some 26 million of them valued at nearly $500,000 had been withdrawn from circulation.

Fractional paper notes had been issued during the war only as an emergency currency. From the first the government intended that they would be replaced by new silver coins as soon as conditions were such that coins would not disappear from circulation. This exchange of new silver coins for fractional notes began to take place in the spring of 1876. It had been authorized more than a year before by the Resumption Act of January 14, 1875. This act directed the Secretary of the Treasury "to coin subsidiary silver and issue it in redemption of fractional notes." Before the end of 1875 more than $9 million in new coins had been minted, and a total of $16 million had been struck before the exchange of coin for the fractional paper actually began in 1876. By that time the price of silver had dropped considerably, and the government had lost money because it had purchased the silver at much higher prices. It was estimated that by the end of October 1877 more than $36 million in the new silver pieces had been minted. They were in such abundance that many of them had to be stored in vaults to keep them out of circulation. But they had served their purpose. So many fractional notes had been redeemed that after 1877 they ceased to be a general currency.

ONE NEW COIN AND TOO MANY OLD ONES

Among the new subsidiary silver coins produced in 1875 was a new denomination, the 20-cent piece (figure 29a). It was authorized by Congress on March 3, 1875. Soon after its appearance, however, the 20-cent piece proved unpopular. People complained that its similarity in design and size to the quarter was confusing. A bill to withdraw the coin, introduced in 1876, finally became a law in 1878. About 1,345,000 of the coins had been struck, mostly in 1875 at the San Francisco and Carson City mints.

With many new silver coins of various denominations in circulation, millions of old subsidiary silver pieces began to reappear from Canada and Latin America. Silver coins had become unpopular everywhere because of a drop in silver prices. Americans unexpectedly found themselves with an oversupply. Those who had been hoarding the old silver coins for many years dumped them into circulation and thus added to the problem. The Treasury immediately halted its production of new subsidiary coins, and by 1880 large amounts of the silver pieces were held in storage.

At first most people were able to dispose of their subsidiary silver coins by purchases of stamps, by payment to government offices, and by bank deposits. But serious problems arose after passage of the Bland-Allison Act of 1878, which created millions of new standard silver dollars. Post offices, for example, refused to accept any 3-cent coins or 20-cent pieces for stamps. Small merchants were overburdened with all kinds of silver coins, and banks began refusing coins for deposits. Storekeepers had to dispose of their surplus to brokers at discounts ranging from 3 per cent to as much as 8 per cent in some sections of the country.

REDEMPTION OF SILVER COINS

To correct these conditions, Congress passed a redemption measure on June 9, 1879. This law made it possible for the Treasury to redeem all subsidiary silver coins, not just those which were in oversupply or unpopular. This was one of the most important steps in creating the modern subsidiary coinage system which the nation enjoys today through the operation of the Federal Reserve System. Today, through the sub-treasuries in this system, coins unwanted in one section of the country can be retired from circulation. They can be held in storage against future demand or distributed through member banks to another section where they may be needed.

Recoinage of worn or uncurrent coins, another big step toward the present system, was authorized by law on March 4, 1900, with the government bearing the cost of recoinage and the inevitable loss in weight of worn coins.

After 1877 a huge stockpile of idle coins—mostly silver dollars but also other silver coins—was held by the Treasury in its vaults. Mintage of half dollars and quarters was limited to a trickle through the late 1870's and 1880's. But from 1890 onward, as growth in population and trade increased, demand for these larger fractional coins resulted in their greatly increased production. Meanwhile, the coinage of dimes, nickels, and cents continued at a brisk pace through the 1870's and 1880's because a great variety of small articles of manufacture—toys, small confections and 2-cent newspapers—stimulated their use.

Among the coins no longer needed was the 3-cent nickel piece, coinage of which was discontinued in 1889. It met the same fate as the unpopular 2-cent bronze and 3-cent silver and half-dime coins, discontinued in 1873. Many Americans had not seen half dimes in their change for many years until in 1877 these coins returned to circulation after use in neighboring countries. People objected to the coin as too closely resembling the dime. They much preferred the 5-cent nickel.

With plenty of silver dollars and paper dollar bills in circulation, there was no further need to mint $1 and $3 gold pieces. Congress dropped these coins from the mintage list by a law passed on September 26, 1890, the same act that officially discontinued the 3-cent nickel. Between the end of the war and 1889, both of the gold coins had been minted in very small quantities. A $4 gold piece called the "Stella," because of the big star engraved on its reverse, was coined only in 1879 and 1880. It was the last denomination to be created in the U.S. coinage system. It is considered a pattern rather than a regular coin. Only a few hundred of the pieces were struck, and all are today classified as numismatic rarities. The law of 1890 was a landmark in our coinage history. It reduced our fractional currency to five denominations, the half dollar, quarter, dime, 5-cent nickel, and 1-cent piece. Up to the present these coins have withstood every test in serving the nation's changing needs in business transactions.

NEW DESIGNS ON COINS

The 1890 law authorized the Treasury Department to change the designs on coins at any time after twenty-five years. There had been only minor changes in the devices on the half dollar, quarter, and dime since Liberty-seated types of these coins appeared in the late 1830's. Charles E. Barber, the chief engraver of the mint from 1880 to 1917, designed the new large Liberty-head types of these pieces (figure 30), which appeared in 1892. Since then they have been commonly referred to as "Barber" coins. The new Liberty-head 5-cent piece, issued in 1883, was also designed by Barber. Unfortunately, he left out the word CENTS on the first issue of the new coins, leaving only the large "V" to indicate the denomination. Dishonest persons gilded some of these 5-cent pieces and passed them off as $5 half eagles. The design of the coin was immediately corrected to include the word CENTS under the "V."

No changes were made in designs on silver dollars or gold coins until much later. The Indian-head cent likewise remained unchanged until 1909.

THE REVIVAL OF SILVER DOLLARS

Attempts by Silverites and silver-mining interests to have the country abandon the gold standard and revert to the old bimetallic or double standard had resulted in passage by Congress of a compromise measure, the Bland-Allison Act of February 28, 1878. This law directed the Secretary of the Treasury to purchase monthly from two million to four million dollars' worth of silver bullion at the market price, to be coined into "standard silver dollars" of the old weight and legal-tender status. The act, passed over the veto of President Rutherford B. Hayes, reinstated the silver dollar. But the measure

*Figure 30. Coins designed by Charles E. Barber. (a)
Liberty-head half dollar, 1892. (b) Liberty-head
dime, 1892. (c) Five-cent piece without the word*
CENTS, *1883. (d) A later issue of the same coin with
the word* CENTS *added.* (American Numismatic Society)

did not permit free coinage, as the free-silver advocates wanted, and had previously been provided
by law. It was not a bimetallic measure. It made
the silver dollar a subsidiary coin, worth less as bullion than as money because of the big drop in the
price of silver. But the silver-mining interests were,
quite naturally, pleased with this means of disposing
of so much of their output.

Only in the West and in the South were the new
silver dollars accepted in large numbers. The West
disliked paper money and also wanted to support
silver. They took to the "cartwheels," as they often
called the dollars, immediately and remained loyal
to them for generations thereafter, at least in certain localities. Until a few years ago, a tourist in
the silver-mining regions of the West might receive
silver dollars in change, instead of dollar bills, to
remind him that he was traveling in "silver country." Greenbacks were not accepted in California
until after their value equaled that of gold, in 1879.
In the South the coins were acceptable, particularly
to recently emancipated slaves, who refused to use
greenbacks, and to others who preferred "hard"
money. But in the North and East people generally
did not want the big heavy dollars. This dislike no
doubt hastened the government's decision to issue
a new type of paper money called "silver certificates," based on silver deposits in the Treasury.
This form of money has until only recently remained
one of the major elements in U.S. currency.

HUGE DOLLAR MINTAGES

More than 378 million silver dollars authorized by the Bland-Allison Act were minted during the first twelve years of issue, according to U.S. Treasury figures. The Sherman Silver Purchase Act of 1890 and subsequent measures resulted in another 192 million of the same coins being struck at the mints by 1904, making a total of 570 million struck in the twenty-six years from 1878 to 1904. Coin collectors commonly refer to these silver dollars as "Morgan" dollars, because they were designed by George T. Morgan, whose initial "M" appears on the neck of the big Liberty head on the coin (figure 31a). Coinage of the dollars was suspended in 1904, when the Treasury's silver bullion supply was exhausted. Under the provisions of the Pittman Act of 1918, coinage was resumed in 1921, when more than 86.7 million more Morgan dollars were made. This was immediately followed by a new issue of 183.5 million "Peace" dollars (figure 31b). This was the last appearance in U.S. coinage of the silver dollar. The denomination was terminated in 1935. The Peace dollar was designed by Anthony de Francisci.

During the entire history of the silver dollar, from 1794 to 1935, a total of 855,611,127 pieces were struck. As late as December 1963, despite meltings and disposal of silver dollars to foreign countries, more than half of the entire mintages remained in the hands of the public, while about 32 million

*Figure 31. (a) Morgan dollar, 1878. (b) Peace dollar, 1921.* (American Numismatic Society)

were held in the Treasury or Federal Reserve bank vaults.

The value of the silver dollar reinstated in 1878 was never dependent on the value of the silver it contained, for metallic value continued to slump during the 1880's and much later. The intrinsic value was 82 cents in 1885, 75 cents in 1889, and as low as 48 cents in 1900. Thus the powerful legislative support silver-mining interests had received proved ineffective. Yet farmers of the South and West, badly hit by the low prices they received for their products in the 1880's, seemed to think that more silver dollars and inflation would free them from the repressive effects of the gold standard. Some Republicans, as well as the Democrats, supported the renewed pressure for bimetallism and inflation. These supporters influenced passage of the Sherman Silver Purchase Act of July 14, 1890, which required the Treasury to buy each month 4.5 million ounces of silver—almost twice the monthly purchase amount stipulated by the Bland-Allison Act. This was to be paid for by a new type of "treasury note" and could be coined into silver dollars. Though coinage was not obligatory, many millions of dollars were struck.

### THE PANIC OF 1893 AND THE GOLD STANDARD

The new treasury notes were made legal tender redeemable in gold or silver, as the Treasury might determine. The Treasury used gold for the redemption. Consequently, its gold reserve fund dropped from $190 million in 1890 to less than the statutory minimum level of $100 million in 1893. Uncertainty gripped the country and brought on the Panic of 1893. President Cleveland, then serving his second term, was a Democrat who believed in the gold standard. He sought repeal of the Sherman Silver Purchase Act, and Congress complied on November 1, 1893. Cleveland subsequently secured new gold supplies for the Treasury.

Notwithstanding the failure of the Sherman Silver

Purchase Act, agitation for bimetallism continued. William Jennings Bryan, an ardent Silverite who became the Democratic candidate for President in 1896, called silver "the paramount issue." In his famous "Cross of Gold" speech at his party's national convention that year he pictured the nation being crucified on "a cross of gold." He meant, of course, the gold standard. Bryan's defeat by William McKinley in the race for the Presidency, decisive in electoral votes but quite close in popular votes, was considered a narrow victory for the forces opposing free silver. In the 1900 election, Bryan again ran for President on a free-silver plank. This time he was decisively defeated by McKinley, who had, as in the previous election, the strong backing of "big business." Silver, it seemed, had by this time become a dead issue. A majority of Congress obviously believed this, for, on March 14, 1900, it passed the Gold Standard Act, which declared the gold dollar to be "the standard unit of value."

The Silverites and sponsors of bimetallism went down to defeat, but not without what seemed to them a just cause for battle. Historians have pointed out that after 1870 the world production of gold, great as it was, did not increase as fast as the world production of goods. This, they claim, restricted the currency supply and drove prices down, not only in the United States but all over the world. Reaction to the lower prices, as has already been noted, took the form of a movement for more abundant and cheaper money during the postwar period. But the worldwide movement toward the gold standard was a powerful factor in favor of the course this nation took. "Free silver, if adopted, would have prolonged uncertainty and placed the United States in a sullen financial position," observed Samuel Eliot Morison in his *History of the American People*. At last this country had come to realize that it could not follow an isolated financial course. It was destined to play a much greater role than ever before in world affairs and the dollar was to be a symbol of its power in the present century. In spite of the importance of silver and various forms of paper money after the Civil War, gold coins had continued to be the major product of U.S. mints. A total of more than $1,350,000,000 in gold coins was struck from 1865 to 1900. More than a billion dollars of this amount was in $20 gold pieces and about $250 million in $10 eagles. Many of these coins were exported to other countries. Most of the remainder was held in bank vaults. Even in America's "Age of Gold," gold coins never circulated to an extent that would impress the general public with their tremendous importance as the basis of paper currencies and in international trade.

# 14

# FINAL YEARS OF THE
# GOLD STANDARD

The twentieth century, particularly since the early
1930's, has witnessed revolutionary changes in U.S.
money. The composition of coins in circulation has
changed greatly. Gold coins were taken out of circulation in 1933 and 1934. More recently silverless
coins were put into circulation. But, far more im-
portantly, the concept and uses of money have
changed. As the United States began to play a leading role in world affairs, its money became more
closely involved than ever before with other world
currencies. Perhaps because America is considered
the dominant power in developed resources, industrial and military might, and national wealth, the
U.S. dollar is today the world's most accepted standard of monetary value. This is true in spite of inflation, devaluation, and metallic changes. In times
past the historic Spanish dollar was valued for its
high silver content. The American dollar, on the
other hand, is today valued not for its intrinsic
*194*

worth in metal, but for the government's ability to back it, whether in coin or paper form.

The twentieth century has not only been an age of prosperity and power for the United States but also a period of monetary abundance increasingly geared to the needs of the sophisticated age. But how different is money today! The vast bulk of money payments are made by checks based on bank deposits and by credit cards for purchases which will later be paid for by check. Nearly 80 per cent of all money consists of commercial bank accounts. Paper currency and coin make up only the remaining 20 per cent. Checks and credit cards have many advantages. They are safe and convenient. Coins and other currency, as one authority observed, now constitute only "the small change of commerce." On the other hand, coins, made by the billions, perform many new duties unheard of at the beginning of the century. They are used increasingly to turn the wheels of all sorts of coin-operated machines, which dispense an unbelievable assortment of goods and services.

THE CENTURY BEGINS ON THE GOLD STANDARD

By 1900 the United States had stepped up production of coins of gold, silver, and smaller denominations to meet the requirements of its expanding population and its agricultural, industrial, and financial growth. The country seemed to be firmly on the gold-coin standard, as were most other major powers with whom it competed in world trade. The bitter political controversies over silver and bimetallism, which had raged in the latter part of the nineteenth century, had gradually subsided. Other domestic problems and new international issues came to the fore.

War with Spain in 1898 resulted in new U.S. possessions and responsibilities in the Caribbean area and in the Philippines and Far East. America became dedicated to a protective, imperialistic policy, particularly in Latin America. Theodore Roosevelt, who suddenly became the chief executive after the assassination of President McKinley in 1901, proved to be the man of the hour. He wielded a "big stick" in international relations when he deemed it necessary and in domestic matters as well. In pursuit of his acclaimed "Square Deal" for every citizen he was occupied with "trust-busting" and regulating big business and with improving the lot of the farmer, laborer, and small-business man. Under Roosevelt the gold standard was further consolidated. Gold was increasingly used to create more new coins and gold-backed paper money called gold certificates. The President himself took a keen interest in creating coins of more beautiful design, specifically the Saint-Gaudens series (1907) of gold coins. The Lincoln-head cent was also conceived during his Administration, though not issued until 1909.

THE COINAGE SYSTEM RESISTS CHANGE

During the period from 1900 to 1933 the U.S. coinage system was not materially modified. There were no metallic changes, though coin design changed and the volume of production rose. The output of gold coins during the prosperous first decade of the century greatly increased, averaging nearly $100 million yearly, but thereafter it declined until the mid-1920's. Gold coins in circulation fell from $612 million in 1914 to about $475 million in 1920. Coinage law, too, remained unchanged, except for the Pittman Act of 1918, which will be discussed later. New demands for increased production of fractional coins from the turn of the century and particularly during the World War I period were promptly met. The Treasury had at last been granted the authority for unlimited coinage by the Attorney General in 1905, after seeking it in vain from Congress during the previous twenty-five years. Particularly pronounced was the demand for the 1-, 5-, 10-, and 25-cent pieces during the war period. Prices were rising and there were new taxes on numerous items, including cigarettes, cosmetics, entertainment, transportation, and other services. There was therefore a greater need for small coins. In fact, the problem of making small change was so great that Congress considered at different times during the period the creation of coins of odd denominations, such as 2½-, 6-, 7-, 8-, and 15-cent pieces. None of these was ever produced.

Because of the great demand for 1-cent pieces, a serious shortage of them developed during the fall of 1917, though the mints were turning out 3 million cent pieces daily by November of that year. Mint director Raymond T. Baker even went so far as to urge children to stop putting pennies in their toy banks. He also suggested the possibility of issuing fractional notes to help relieve the shortage. The sale of war savings certificates, however, brought millions of cents into the Treasury, and increased minting of cent pieces helped solve the problem. New cents totaled some 370 million in 1918, 590 million in 1919, and more than 400 million in 1920.

THE SILVER SHORTAGE

Despite the extraordinary demand for all types of silver coins and 5-cent pieces, no serious shortage developed. But there was a severe shortage of silver, which was needed for various purposes during the war period. Pure silver, which had sold at around 50 cents an ounce in New York in 1915, rose to 84 cents in 1917, to 98 cents in 1918, and to an average price of $1.12 in 1919. In November of that year the price, amid extreme fluctuations, reached a peak of $1.38¼ in the East and went to even higher levels in the San Francisco area. At the $1.38¼ level, for example, the pure silver contained in four quarters or ten dimes was worth about $1.

This tremendous rise in the value of pure silver naturally threatened to drive all the coins off the market. Thus, in late 1919 and early 1920, the country was on the verge of a complete collapse of its subsidiary silver currency, similar to the one experienced in 1862 during the Civil War, when retail trade became paralyzed by the sudden loss of silver coins from circulation. Fortunately, however, this did not occur in the immediate post-World War I period; the price of silver began dropping to safer levels, relieving Treasury officials of the necessity of coping with a situation for which they seemed to have no solution. Belatedly, in December 1919 a bill was introduced in Congress to reduce the weight of silver coins, rather than to decrease the amount of pure silver and increase the proportion of copper, as was done in the Coinage Act of 1965. The proposal was forgotten in a Congressional committee as the price of silver began to drop.

SALE OF SILVER DOLLARS

The United States, holding vast amounts of silver dollars in its vaults, did not mint any of these coins from 1904 to 1921. During the war period, however, the rising price of silver and the urgent demand for silver for coinage in India enabled the United States to dispose of a large part of its silver-dollar surplus at a handsome profit. Under the Pittman Act of April 23, 1918, the United States would sell silver, obtained from melting down the coins into bullion form, at $1 an ounce to the British government, which then ruled India. When these coins had been minted, the price of silver was far less. Of the total of 270 million that had been melted down, the U.S. government sold some 259 million to Britain for shipment to India and used about 11 million to furnish metal for minting smaller U.S. silver coins.

The Pittman Act contained a provision that proved highly profitable for American silver interests, who evidently had a strong hand in passing the act. It provided that a number of new silver dollars equal in value to the dollars melted down—270 million—had to be coined from silver purchased by the U.S. government from American mine owners. Between 1921 and 1933, when the new dollars were struck, the price of silver on the open market had dropped considerably. It was selling at 63 cents an ounce in 1921 and at 67 cents in 1924, during the period when most of the coins were struck.

NEW AND ATTRACTIVE DESIGNS FOR COINS

According to the Treasury Department, "selection of design for our coins is made by the Director of the Mint with the approval of the Secretary of the Treasury." Congress has, in a few instances, prescribed a coin design. An example is a design by New York sculptor John Flanagan for the Washington Bicentennial 25-cent piece issued from 1932 to the present, which bears the portrait of the first U.S. President. Except where Congress determines otherwise, the design on a coin may be changed only once in 25 years.

About 86.7 million of the silver dollars struck in

1921 were of the old Morgan design, while the remaining 183.5 million struck from 1921 to 1933 were of the new Peace-dollar design created by Anthony de Francisci to commemorate peace between the United States and Germany. About 7 million Peace dollars were struck in 1934 and 1935, as provided by the Thomas Amendment to the Agricultural Adjustment Act of May 1933.

New and artistically attractive designs were given to other coins during the decade between 1907 and 1916, when a number of prominent artists took part in creating the "new look" for modern coinage. One of these artists, the famous Irish-born sculptor Augustus Saint-Gaudens, created in 1907 the designs for both the $20 gold double-eagle and the $10 eagle pieces (figure 32), hailed as a new high standard in coinage art. It is interesting to note that the motto IN GOD WE TRUST was left off the $20 and $10 gold pieces in 1907, but, at the insistence of Congress, was restored in 1908.

Commemorating the centenary of Lincoln's birth, artist Victor D. Brenner designed a new 1-cent piece (figure 32d), which appeared in 1909, replacing the Indian-head 1-cent piece in use since 1859. In 1913, James Earle Fraser, world-renowned sculptor and student of Saint-Gaudens, created the Buffalo nickel (figure 33). The Indian-head face on this coin was modeled after three different Indians, one of whom was Chief Iron Tail, who fought General Custer in the battle of the Little Big Horn in 1876. In 1916,

*Figure 32.* (a) *Saint-Gaudens ten-dollar "eagle,"*
*1907.* (b) *The same piece with the motto* IN GOD
WE TRUST *added, 1920.* (c) *Saint-Gaudens twenty-*
*dollar "double eagle."* (d) *Lincoln-head cent, 1909.*
(American Numismatic Society)

Adolph Weinman designed the Mercury-head dime and also the Liberty-walking half dollar (figure 34), and Harmon A. MacNeil created the Liberty-standing quarter. These three new types replaced the Liberty-head design of Charles E. Barber, chief engraver of the mint, which first appeared on the coins in 1892.

ARTIST RECOGNITION

For more than a century it has been the custom for artists who create new coin designs to have their initials placed inconspicuously on the piece. The initials are to be found at various locations on the face or on the reverse of the coin, and in tiny letters that sometimes require a magnifying glass to detect. For example, in the case of some 1864 bronze cents, the mint's engraver, Longacre, placed his initial, "L," on the ribbon of the wreath on the reverse. In the case of the Lincoln cent, Brenner's initials, "V. D. B.," appeared much more legibly beneath the wreath on the reverse of the first 1909 pieces. Consequently, Secretary of the Treasury Franklin MacVeigh objected and argued that only the letter "B" should be shown. But the necessary change was found to be impossible if production schedules were to be met, and the solution was to erase all three letters from the die. No initials of any kind were shown on subsequent issues until the controversial matter was finally resolved in 1918 by restoring the initials "V. D. B." to Lincoln's shoulder, near the edge of the coin. In

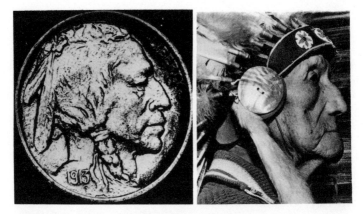

*Figure 33. (a) Buffalo nickel designed by James Earle Fraser, 1913. (b) Chief Iron Tail, one of the models for the face of the Buffalo nickel.* (Wide World Photos)

1959 the artist Frank Gasparro designed the Lincoln-Memorial reverse for the cent. Both of his initials appear at the right of the base of the steps leading into the memorial structure.

### THE FEDERAL RESERVE SYSTEM

Although U.S. coins changed very little between 1900 and 1933, the nation's monetary system as a whole went through considerable reformation and improvement early in the period. Most of the changes involved paper money. A new kind of legal-tender paper currency was issued, known as Federal Reserve notes, which has become the principal paper currency in circulation today. But by far the most important advance was the Federal Reserve System. It was created by the Federal Reserve Act of 1913. This law gave the government a controlling hand in the management of the monetary system, which had previously been too much subject to control by the "money interests." The idea of a central bank for controlling money and banking was not new. The Bank of England had been operating since 1694. The First and Second Banks of the United States had been chartered by the federal government, with authorization to combine the functions of central and private banking, though their powers were greatly limited. Those institutions had not been revived after President Jackson refused to renew the charter of the Second Bank of the United States in 1836. The federal government had re-entered the monetary system in 1864 by enacting the National Bank Act; this law had regulated those functions of the national banks involved with banking and currency issuing. But this government control had not been enough to prevent the panics of 1873, 1893, and 1907.

Before the establishment of the Federal Reserve System, currency was based largely on gold and consisted principally of gold certificates, gold coin, greenbacks, and bond-secured notes. A great part of the reserves in small banks were on deposit with banks in the great money centers, known as central reserve cities, such as New York and Chicago. The small banks kept cash reserves amounting to only about 15 per cent of their deposits. The large banks in the reserve centers held about 25 per cent in cash.

*Figure 34. (a) Mercury-head dime design by Adolph Weinman, 1916. (b) Weinman's "Liberty-walking" half dollar, 1916.* (American Numismatic Society)

But in emergencies, such as "runs" on banks when depositors demanded their money, cash could not be made available in time to prevent banks from closing their doors. A chain reaction resulted, and runs spread to other banks, depleting their cash and creating panic. In some cases these panics brought distress to millions of people and affected the whole national economy.

THE PANIC OF 1907

The Panic of 1907, interrupting a period of national prosperity, was triggered by the failure of a few banks and trust companies involved in speculation. It was not a disastrous panic of long duration, but it aroused the nation to do something about curing the ills in its antiquated monetary system.

In 1908, during President William Howard Taft's Administration, Congress set up a National Monetary Commission, headed by Senator Nelson Aldrich of Rhode Island, to investigate the banking and currency system and propose needed changes. The commission found that in times of crisis there were insufficient reserves in the banks and lack of cooperation among them. There was no means of increasing or decreasing the supply of money in response to the business needs of the country. There was no central control of banking practices. And lastly, there was too much concentration of banking capital in New York City. Corrective measures proposed by the commission included the formation of a "National Reserve Association" based on a number of regional associations. But it remained for the Federal Reserve Act passed during President Woodrow Wilson's Administration to embody much of the proposed legislation and to make the banking and monetary system more responsive to national needs.

COMPOSITION OF THE FEDERAL RESERVE SYSTEM

Without detailing the complex functions of the Federal Reserve System, we will here only point out briefly its composition and important operations. It is composed of:

1. A Federal Reserve Board in Washington composed of seven members or "governors." Each

member is appointed by the President of the United States, with the consent of the Senate, for a fourteen-year term.

2. A Federal Open Market Committee composed of the seven Federal Reserve Board members, plus five representatives of the twelve Federal Reserve regional banks. This committee, which also meets in Washington, was added in 1933 and 1934 to strengthen the emergency powers of the Board in adjusting money supply to meet varying business conditions.

3. The twelve regional Federal Reserve banks, strategically located in as many large cities over the country, and private and commercial "member" banks, which today number more than six thousand. All national banks are required to join their respective regional Federal Reserve bank, and other banks may also join. Although today more than half of the banks of the country are not part of this system, the member banks are said to account for about 85 per cent of all bank deposits. The money reserves needed by each bank are determined by the Board of Governors. This board exercises general supervision over the Federal Reserve banks and supervises and regulates the issue and retirement of Federal Reserve notes (paper currency) .

The Federal Open Market Committee has great policy-making powers. It controls money supply, credit, and interest rates. Section 12A of the Federal

Reserve Act, as amended, states: "No Federal Reserve bank shall engage in or decline to engage in open market operations under section 14 of this act except in accordance with the direction of and regulations adopted by the Committee." ("Open market" concerns the buying and selling of securities by the Federal Reserve banks.) The committee, "subject to review and determination of the Board of Governors," sets "rates of discount to be charged by the Federal Reserve banks for each class of paper."

## MAJOR FUNCTIONS OF THE FEDERAL RESERVE SYSTEM

The ability of commercial member banks to create needed money and credit has been a major function of the Federal Reserve System from the beginning. The reserves of member banks are concentrated in the regional Federal Reserve bank for emergency use, such as a run on a member bank. The F.R.S. also helps local banks meet requests for loans with the flexible currency of Federal Reserve notes. Before the system was established, local banks often lacked funds to give perfectly sound loans to businessmen and farmers. Without such loans the businessman's factory might close and the farmer's crop might rot for lack of necessary machinery. The new money is put into circulation when the local bank brings a businessman's promissory note to the regional F.R.S. bank and receives Federal Reserve notes in return. For this privilege, local banks pay the Federal Reserve bank a small fee, known as a "rediscount" fee, the amount of which can change from time to time as a means of controlling the creation of new money. These regional banks are really "banks for bankers," dealing only with member banks, not with individual depositors.

Besides creating new paper money, the Federal Reserve Board acts as fiscal (financial) agent for the federal government, issuing all the government's notes and bonds. It also clears checks for member banks and distributes money to them, coin as well as paper. Though the U.S. Mint in the Treasury Department produces the nation's coins, the amount and proportion of various denominations made available in each locality is largely determined by the regional Federal Reserve bank.

INDEPENDENT STATUS OF THE
FEDERAL RESERVE SYSTEM

Under the Constitution the power to create all forms of money belongs to Congress, yet the Federal Reserve System creates the country's paper money. Congress delegated this power in the Federal Reserve Act of 1913 to the Federal Reserve Board because in emergencies it is able to act more quickly and effectively than is Congress. The members of the board are also experts in monetary matters, about which most Congressmen have only limited knowledge. Thus, the board has a fearful amount of power. By putting money into circulation or taking it out, by creating credit, and by raising or lowering interest rates, it exercises a controlling power over the nation's economy.

The policy-making power of the Federal Reserve officials is independent of Congress. They neither require nor necessarily seek the approval of any other branch of government. The actions of the Federal Open Market Committee may at times even run counter to the wishes of the government in power, for example, in setting interest rates. For this reason the Committee is often criticized as being "too conservative" or as favoring the banks or "money interests" rather than the interests of the nation as a whole. Nevertheless, the Federal Reserve System has been a bulwark in stabilizing and streamlining the nation's monetary system. In spite of this fact, as will be discussed later, the system established in 1913 was not able to prevent the biggest economic collapse the nation has ever experienced—the Great Depression of the 1930's.

INFLUENCE OF WORLD WAR I ON MONEY

World War I resulted in upsetting the available resources and money supply of the major European powers. Although it was also costly for the United States, the war was responsible for vaulting America into the commanding position of a world power. Early in the conflict gold flowed into the United States from the European Allies on an unprecedented scale in payment for needed supplies and materials. This gold movement led to a considerable increase in the gold holdings of the Federal Reserve System. By the end of 1918 the country's stocks of gold equaled about 40 per cent of the world's known gold reserves. On the other hand, England, France, and other European nations had to abandon the gold standard because of substantial gold losses and depleted treasuries. The United States, however, continued on the gold-coin standard until the 1930's. With some $10 billion in loans, it helped the Allies to maintain their weakened monetary systems. As a result of the war the American dollar became the world's leading monetary unit, backed by increasingly large reserves and a newly attained strong credit position.

The war also contributed to an extremely heavy demand for paper money, as well as for coins. This was caused by the expansion of business and employment and the necessity of facilitating the government's war loans. Federal Reserve notes became the principal currency, increasing from $507 million in 1917 to $1.7 billion in 1918 and to $3 billion in 1920. At the same time circulation of both gold and silver certificates was temporarily reduced. Gold certificates were largely taken out of circulation and transferred from member banks to the Federal Reserve regional banks to serve as additional security for Federal Reserve notes. However, a few years later, as business conditions became normal, the Federal Reserve System placed a large number of gold certificates into circulation. When this currency rose from $259 million in 1920 to $1 billion in 1925, the yellow bills were to be found in many American pockets. Also during the 1920's the U.S. Mint turned out nearly $1 billion in gold coins and many of these also went into circulation. The American people had no hint that they were then living in the final years of gold money.

The nation's wartime boom had skyrocketed prices and the cost of living, roughly doubling 1913 prices. This boom was followed by a brief recession in 1920–1921, though prices remained more than 50 per cent above the prewar level. A period of apparent prosperity soon followed and continued through the "Roaring Twenties." Suddenly, in 1929, a stock market crash signaled that something was wrong in the operation of the country's economy.

PROSPERITY AND THE CRASH

In many ways the "Golden Twenties" were fabulous years long to be remembered by the American people. Never before had so many Americans enjoyed such heights of business prosperity, good wages, and a high standard of living as under the Republican administrations of Warren G. Harding, Calvin Coolidge, and Herbert Hoover. Production of goods rose to new record levels with corresponding increases in national wealth. New industries sprang up overnight to produce new conveniences and comforts. There was more leisure and entertainment for large segments of the population, which had grown from about 76 million in 1900 to 105.7 million in 1920, and to 122.7 million in 1930.

The twenties were years remarkable for the development of communications and entertainment media—radio broadcasting, the "talking" motion picture, television, and overseas telephone service. It was the age of mass production of automobiles and the decade in which Charles A. Lindbergh's famous New York to Paris flight of 1927 heralded the beginnings of overseas air travel. Women won the right to vote in 1920 with the passage of the Nineteenth Amendment, as well as other freedoms.

Millions of people were also investment-minded during the twenties. They wanted to get rich overnight by playing the stock market. This speculative mania had been encouraged to the point of danger in a number of ways. With the growing power and resources of business corporations, there was wider distribution of ownership shares in corporate enterprises. The expansion and consolidation of business enterprises from 1919 to 1929 often concealed, even from the financially expert, the fact that industrial prosperity was based largely on speculation. People were guided more by stock quotations than by profit-and-loss statements of business concerns. Installment buying had become widespread and so had the habit of buying stocks on thin margins.

Here one may ask the question: What had become of the Federal Reserve System? Was it not supposed to have control over such speculative developments?

Strangely enough, such problems seem to have been simply ignored. Instead of reducing the money supply in order to check speculation and stock price inflation, the Federal Reserve System allowed its member banks to expand credit. They created money by making loans to brokers who offered security in the form of already inflated stocks. Brokers' loans grew from $2 billion to $8 billion during the boom period of the late twenties.

In contrast to the previous era, which had concerned itself with trust-busting, the twenties were marked by a laissez-faire approach. The government refrained from regulating business practices, and controls were almost nonexistent. But the day of reckoning came. It dawned on October 23, 1929, when prices on the "Big Board" of the New York Stock Exchange and other exchanges dropped sharply —and continued to drop until November 13. Recovery followed, but it was only temporary. The downward movement, wavering upward at times, finally hit rock bottom in mid-1932.

Historians have pointed out that the collapse of the stock market did not in itself cause, but rather triggered, the general economic collapse. Although the causes of the so-called Great Depression are too numerous to be discussed in this book, a few can be mentioned: the depressed condition of agriculture throughout the entire decade, overproduction of manufactured goods, installment buying, the failure of purchasing power to keep up with productivity, and the effect of depressions in other countries on the U.S. economy. Many corrective steps were taken, a few by President Hoover and many bolder ones under the "New Deal" of President Franklin D. Roosevelt, beginning in 1933. But in many respects the Great Depression was only completely relieved by the nation's rearmament in 1939–1940 for World War II.

# 15

## THE MOVEMENT AWAY FROM GOLD AND SILVER

The stock market crash had badly shaken the spirit of optimism and overconfidence that had pervaded the twenties, but for some time after the crash, many people were still hopeful of recovery. Gradually the mood changed to deep pessimism, if not despair. Most people came to the point not only of losing confidence in banks but also of distrusting the value of the paper currency that for so long had been regarded as good as gold. People began to demand payments in gold, creating runs on banks all over the country.

In March 1933 stock prices had dropped to about one-sixth of the late 1929 level. Among the existing 24,079 banks in the country, 1,352 had suspended payments in 1930. In 1931 the number of failures rose to 2,294, followed by an additional 1,456 failures in 1932. By March 1933, another 408 banks had closed their doors (figure 35). The people's general feeling of distress had been aggravated in 1932 by the campaign preceding the Presidential election, in which

*Figure 35. A bank president announces closing of the bank's doors, early 1930's.* (Wide World Photos)

both Democrats and Republicans accused each other of responsibility for the depression.

Depositors' runs on banks started early in 1932, at first slowly, but soon with increased speed and pressure. In the beginning people were content to draw out Federal Reserve notes and other paper money. But gradually they started to draw from the limited gold supply kept by banks as backing for paper money. If they could not get gold, they wanted gold certificates. In many states bank holidays were declared to ward off further bank failures. "Barter" organizations were created, and scrip was issued and circulated by municipalities as local substitutes for legal currency. The hoarding of gold coins and other preferred forms of money was quite evident during the early part of 1933. President Roosevelt declared a national bank holiday on March 6, 1933, just two days after taking office.

Banks all over the country were closed during the bank holiday "to permit readjustment of our financial system," as the President proclaimed, and to inspire confidence in the system. The holiday, intended to end March 9, was extended to March 12. The banks were forbidden to transact any business and were especially prohibited from paying out any coin, bullion, or currency, except by special permission of the Secretary of the Treasury.

Immediately following the end of the bank holiday, between nine thousand and ten thousand banks, including nearly all of the large metropolitan institutions, were allowed to open without restrictions. Another five thousand banks reopened with restrictions on the amounts which depositors might withdraw, and between three thousand and four thousand banks were placed in the hands of conservators, who might or might not liquidate them upon further examination. The number of banks definitely and finally closed was estimated at more than one thousand. Some banks survived through consolidation with other banks. Introduction of Federal Deposit Insurance by the Banking Act of June 1933 greatly strengthened the position of banks.

### STEPS IN NATIONALIZATION OF GOLD

The disappearance of gold into the hands of hoarders and its exportation to other countries required immediate action by the federal government. One of the provisions of the Emergency Banking Act passed by Congress on March 9, 1933, was that the Secretary of the Treasury should require every person to turn in gold coin, gold bullion, and gold certificates for an "equivalent amount" of other currency. This proved to be one of the first steps toward the nationalization of gold and the abandonment of the gold-coin standard, though it was not until April that the President declared that the nation was going off the gold standard. On the following day, March 10, the President prohibited by executive order the export of gold and gold certificates to other countries, except under license of the Secretary of the Treasury.

The Banking Act, which helped greatly to restore public confidence in banking, caused bank deposits, including gold, to be returned to a large extent to the banks. The gold later went into the vaults of the Treasury.

### DOLLAR DEVALUATION AND INFLATION

In the swift-moving drama of monetary change, the Agricultural Adjustment Act of May 12, 1933, was of particular national and international interest. The act was aimed at helping the farmer and the unemployed (about 13 million people at that time, or about triple the number of unemployed in 1930)

*Figure 36. Unemployed workers standing in a "bread line" in the 1930's.* (Wide World Photos)

(figure 36). The Thomas Amendment to this act showed the strong hand of the inflationists in Congress. It granted the President the unprecedented power to reduce the amount of gold in the dollar (still based on gold) by as much as 50 per cent. This step was declared necessary in order to stabilize domestic prices, which had dropped considerably during the depression. Moreover, it would place the nation in a better competitive position in relation to foreign countries that had already gone off the gold standard. With their depreciated currencies these countries could undersell American producers. England and Germany were among a number of such countries that had resumed the gold standard in the 1920's but had abandoned it in the early 1930's.

Congress had left the matter of devaluing the dollar largely to the President, hoping that he might, in consultation with other major powers, arrive at some satisfactory international agreement. But with the United States now definitely headed toward inflation, the World Economic and Monetary Conference in London in June 1933 found such an agreement impossible. Meanwhile, the steps already taken by the United States in abandoning the gold standard and inflating prices had had some success, but not enough for the Administration. The gold ratio of the devalued dollar had to be decided upon definitely, and soon.

### THE GOLD RESERVE ACT

On January 30, 1934, Congress passed the Gold Reserve Act as the new basis for the American monetary system. It specified that "no gold shall thereafter be coined [the last was coined in 1933], and no gold shall hereafter be paid out or delivered by the United States. . . . All gold coins of the United States shall be withdrawn from circulation, and together with all other gold owned by the United States, shall be formed into bars of such weight and degree of fineness as the Secretary of the Treasury may direct." Gold held by the Federal Reserve banks was to be surrendered to the government in return for dollars worth the amount of gold corresponding to the new weight of the dollar as proclaimed by the President. That weight was to be no more than 60 per cent of its previous statutory weight.

THE DOLLAR DEVALUED

The gold standard was abandoned as part of the Administration's plan to raise prices in the United States in order to counteract the Depression. The first step was to devalue the dollar—that is, to hold less than a dollar's worth of gold as security for a paper or silver dollar. Specifically, the amount of gold backing for the dollar was reduced from 23.22 grains to 13.71 grains. This meant that the dollar in 1932 became worth only 59 cents in gold.

The government's action was based on the "quantity theory" of money, to which the Greenbackers and Populists had been so devoted in the nineteenth century. They thought that the amount of money in circulation could be increased by devaluing other currency in relation to gold. The idea was that if the amount of gold represented by the dollar were decreased, foreign powers would not wish to accept the dollar in payment of debts. If they would accept it in return for goods in international trade, they would demand more goods instead. This demand would force the increase of exports of American goods. These goods would therefore become scarce in the United States and their price would go up. This would bring about the inflation hoped for to counteract depression conditions.

There would be another desirable effect of devaluing the dollar. Since it now needed to be represented by only 13.71 grains of gold, there would be a 40.94 per cent reduction in the amount of gold needed to back the dollar. The difference between the old and new weights would mean profit for the government. This "gold profit" on the amount of U.S. currency in circulation at the time the new law went into effect amounted to $2 billion.

THE USE OF GOLD TODAY

Most provisions of the Gold Reserve Act of 1934 have continued in force to the present time. There are no longer any gold coins in circulation in the United States. Private ownership of gold is still illegal, except for special purposes authorized by the Secretary of the Treasury. For example, members of coin clubs and numismatic groups are allowed, for historical and numismatic purposes, to keep gold coins in their collections. The Secretary of the Treasury has considerable discretion in the matter of buying and selling gold. He is permitted, but not required, to sell gold in bullion form for "professional, industrial, and artistic use," and for the purpose of settling international balances. He may buy or sell gold at any price he chooses. But in actual practice, the various Secretaries of the Treasury since 1934 have bought and sold gold at $35 an ounce and, when necessary, have freely exported gold at that price.

A sudden halt in unrestricted sale of gold by the

U.S. came, however, on March 17, 1968. To stem speculative purchases of the metal, which threatened to deplete the national reserves and those of certain western European powers allied in mutual currency support, the U.S. and these nations came to an agreement to freeze their existing gold holdings for their own official uses. This, in effect, created a "two-price" system: $35 an ounce for gold in government dealings among these nations (and others that might join them); and any price that supply and demand establishes for private purchases of gold in the U.S. and abroad. As a result of this agreement, today the U.S. dollar can be exchanged for gold only by foreign governments for monetary purposes (not for speculation).

Since the United States no longer has gold coins in circulation, but still has a "gold dollar unit" defined by law, one may ask: What sort of a gold standard, if any, have we had since 1934? It has been called the "gold management standard," for it is controlled by the U.S. Treasury. Since the Secretary of the Treasury could refuse to sell gold any day he found it necessary, the present standard varies in a flexible manner to meet conditions as they change. It might be called, in the words of former Secretary of the Treasury Henry Morgenthau, Jr., a "24-hour gold standard." This standard functions primarily as an international means of payment, for today the dollar can be exchanged for gold only in restricted international transactions for the adjustment of international payments. While their gold is used abroad, Americans at home no longer have any kind of gold standard, but rather what has been called a "managed paper standard."

The quantity of gold held by the U.S. Treasury has varied greatly through the years since 1934. When the price of gold was arbitrarily raised to $35 an ounce by the United States in the process of devaluing the dollar, much gold was brought into the Treasury from abroad. The U.S. stock of about $7 billion in gold in 1934 rose to above $17 billion in 1939. Much of this gold was to provide dollars to buy war goods. Following World War II gold poured out of Europe, and U.S. stocks of it continued to rise, reaching the $24.8 billion mark in 1949. Since then, however, and particularly since 1957, American gold stocks have declined, reflecting an adverse balance in international transactions. The nation's gold, mostly kept by the Treasury in bullion (bar) form at Fort Knox, Kentucky, amounted to about $10.5 billion in April 1968. At that time $13.6 billion of gold (mostly in bullion form) owned by foreign countries was kept in the vaults of the New York Federal Reserve Bank in New York City. This is the official U.S. bank for handling foreign accounts. The gold is kept there for convenient transferral from one nation's possession to another's. (Much of this gold was at one time owned by the United States.) The gold changes hands physically, as well as in the account books, from one nation to another. The metal bars are removed from the vault of the debtor nation, weighed on a mammoth and highly accurate official scale, and then placed in the vault of the creditor nation. The whole transaction takes place within the same building. This has been found to be the most convenient and inexpensive method for various nations to settle their international balances.

Gold is still the most acceptable form of international money. But there is simply not enough of it to meet the needs of business. Today the United States is the only nation that promises to redeem its own currency in gold—although this promise is limited to international transactions. It cannot be said that the value of the dollar is dependent upon gold; but gold is used in support of the American dollar, which has become an international kind of currency. Primarily, the value of the dollar rests on the capacity of the United States to produce goods and services—that is, on the health of the nation's economy.

THE INTERNATIONAL MONETARY FUND

The international importance of the dollar was greatly enhanced in the World War II period through cooperative steps taken by the United States and other nations of the free world to recover from the costly conflict, even before it ended. The U.S. government's wartime expenses totaled the stupendous figure of $281 billion, or more than five times what World War I had cost. But the U.S. economy remained vigorous, while the other Allies and former enemies were far more financially upset. Restrictions on trade and credit, it was assumed, would greatly hamper the world's recovery, unless corrective action was taken. So, before the war ended, the representatives of forty-four nations of the free world met and planned ahead. This meeting took place in July 1944, at Bretton Woods, New Hampshire. As a result, in December 1946, the International Monetary Fund (I.M.F.) was established. Each nation was allotted a quota to pay into the fund, based on its financial capacity. Each member nation could obtain loans from the fund when needed to help adjust its balance of international payments, "without resorting to measures destructive of national or international prosperity."

The fund, and its associated "World Bank" (the International Bank for Reconstruction and Development), has since been of great financial help to many nations. It is significant that the quotas for payments into the I.M.F. were reckoned in terms of dollars, though all currencies of the participating nations (now numbering more than 100) are used. The U.S. quota in the fund, about 25 per cent of the total, was $5,160,000,000 as of June 1968. Of this, 25 per cent is paid in gold, and the nation's voting power in the fund is restricted to that proportion. Though the I.M.F. is not a part of the United Nations, founded in 1948, it has cooperative connections with the U.N.

BIMETALLISM REVIVED

The Great Depression had left the United States with only six coin denominations—the silver dollar, half dollar, quarter, dime, 5-cent nickel, and cent. It seemed reasonable that with the departure of gold coins, the silver question would be revived. It was, in fact, by the Silverites in Congress who influenced the enactment of laws in 1933 and 1934 to renew a kind of bimetallism. This was done by expanding the government's purchases of silver, which was used for coinage, as backing for more silver certificates, and for monetary reserves. The aim was to have one-fourth of the nation's monetary stocks in silver.

The 1933 Thomas Amendment to the Agricultural Adjustment Act had declared that all coins and currencies were legal tender, with no limitation for silver coins or those of baser metals. It also authorized the President to establish bimetallism with unlimited coinage, based on a gold-silver ratio to be determined by him or by international agreement. The President, however, let this provision of the law lapse without use. He also never complied with the aim of the Silver Purchase Act, passed by Congress on June 19, 1934, to have one-quarter of the nation's monetary stocks in silver. He did, however, purchase large quantities of silver, particularly for backing silver certificates. Circulation of silver certificates rose from $361 million in 1933 to $705 million in 1935, and to $1,230 million in 1938. The denominations of these notes most frequently found in circulation were $1, $2, $5, and $10. Recently, silver shortages have made gradual retirement of this paper money series a necessity.

President Roosevelt took little advantage of the Silver Purchase Act's provision for coining silver dollars. Only about 7 million of the new Peace dollars were struck in 1934 and 1935. These proved to be the last mintages of the silver dollar, despite repeated efforts since then to have more of them struck.

Though most people disliked silver dollars as change, circulation of "cartwheels" rose from about $30 million in 1934 to $39 million in 1938. Meanwhile, the subsidiary silver coins, the dime, quarter, and half-dollar pieces, grew in circulation from $280 million in 1934 to $342 million in 1938, and to $361 million in 1939. This reflected not only an improvement in living standards as the nation recovered from the Depression, but also a greatly increased use of coins in vending machines. Later, during the World War II period of increased currency needs, circulation of silver dollars rose from $46 million in 1940 to $125 million in 1945, while subsidiary silver pieces grew in circulation from $384 million in 1940 to $788 million in 1945.

No 5-cent pieces and very few cent pieces were minted in 1932 and 1933, but from 1935 onward a much greater volume of these coins was struck. The first U.S. coin to be issued in quantities of a billion or more a year was the cent in 1941, when more than

1.1 billion were minted. Since then the yearly mint-age of cents has averaged considerably above the billion mark. There have also been marked increases in the number of nickels, dimes, and quarters struck since the end of World War II.

WARTIME METALLIC CHANGES

Noteworthy metallic changes occurred in certain cent and 5-cent pieces struck during the war years. Zinc-coated steel cent pieces were first minted in 1943 and are occasionally seen in circulation today. Due to a shortage of copper in that critical war year, the Treasury Department resorted to this unusual composition. Subsequently in 1944 and 1945, cents were coined from more than 2 billion copper shell cases salvaged from war surplus. Zinc-coated steel cents soon deteriorated in appearance with wear, but the "shell-case" cents were only slightly dif-ferent in color from the regular bronze pieces, and proved satisfactory in every respect.

A wartime shortage resulted in complete elimina-tion of nickel from the Jefferson 5-cent pieces struck from October 1942 through 1945 (figure 37a). These pieces were 56 per cent copper, 35 per cent silver, and 9 per cent manganese, instead of the regu-lar composition of 75 per cent copper and 25 per cent nickel. The wartime pieces can be readily distin-guished from the others by their mintmarks. All of them had larger than usual mintmark letters, placed above the dome of Monticello, Jefferson's home,

*Figure 37. Memorial coins. (a) Jefferson five-cent piece, 1942. (b) Roosevelt dime, 1946. (c) Franklin-Liberty-Bell half dollar, 1948. (d) Kennedy half dollar, 1964.* (American Numismatic Society)

shown on the reverse of the coin. The letter "P," which denotes the Philadelphia Mint, was used for the first time on this coin to indicate the metallic change.

NEW MEMORIAL COINS

As a memorial to President Roosevelt, who died in 1945, the mints in 1946 began turning out the new Roosevelt dime (figure 37b). It was designed by John R. Sinnock and featured a portrait of the President on its face. Two years later the same artist designed the Franklin-Liberty-Bell half dollar (figure 37c), replacing the Liberty-standing half dollar. Then in 1964, the year following the assassination of President John F. Kennedy, the Kennedy half dollar appeared (figure 37d). Gilroy Roberts, former chief sculptor of the U.S. Mint, designed the portrait of the deceased President. Frank Gasparro, head engraver of the mint, designed the reverse of the coin, on which appeared the Presidential coat of arms and stars representing all fifty states of the Union. This has proved to be the most popular coin ever issued by the United States. Hundreds of millions have been struck in both the old 90 per cent silver and the "clad" 40 per cent silver compositions. But because so many have become keepsakes, they have only occasionally been seen in circulation.

COINAGE CRISIS OF THE 1960'S

Silver has long been one of the most uncertain and

temperamental elements in U.S. coinage. Prices paid for the metal in the "open" or world market have fluctuated from one extreme to another. Through the years these price changes have greatly affected U.S. silver coins, threatening at times to drive them out of circulation, as was pointed out in the previous chapters. It seems to have been the policy of the national government, regardless of the political party in power, to pay domestic silver producers higher prices for the metal than those in the open market. This practice of subsidizing domestic producers sometimes resulted in national scandal. Although threatened with shortage before, there somehow always seemed to be more than enough silver for industry and coinage until the development, in the 1960's, of still another silver crisis. Then it seemed that silver might be driven out of coinage for good.

The background of this situation can be seen in the continuing rise and fall of silver prices in the open market. In 1879, for instance, the price of silver in the New York market went as high as $1.67 an ounce, though the average price that year was $1.12. That was during a period when the U.S. was minting a tremendous number of silver dollars, thus creating a large demand for silver. Thereafter, a downward price trend developed, reaching a low of 47 cents an ounce in 1902. The price rose to $1.38 an ounce in 1919 and 1920, due to a temporary silver shortage. During the depths of the Great Depression in 1932 and 1933, silver sold as low as 24 cents an ounce.

The price level remained between 34 cents and 46 cents an ounce during the next decade, including most of the World War II period. However, unexpected demands for silver arose out of war needs. The Treasury was authorized to sell silver, at first for military purposes, then, following the war, for manufacturing use. With new demands for the metal, which had sold in the open market at 45 cents an ounce in 1944, silver suddenly jumped to almost 71 cents in 1945 and to 90 cents in 1946.

The almost continuous rise in silver prices since World War II has been attributed largely to the growth and expansion of silver-consuming industries, such as those related to photography and electronics and new industries born of the war effort. Increased demands for silver not only caught up with the available supply, but surpassed it around 1959. Realization of this fact hastened the rise in demand and price in the early 1960's. Hoarding of silver coins and speculation in silver occurred, old habits which began to grip the nation anew, threatening extinction of our silver coinage and causing the federal government to apply one emergency measure after another to solve the problem.

Silver coins began disappearing into the hands of hoarders and speculators in 1962 and vanished more rapidly in 1963 and 1964. Banks and mercantile establishments began paying bonuses for fractional coins. Vending machine companies, now among the greatest users of coins, also began hoarding coins because they feared that the situation might grow worse. In June 1964, Assistant Secretary of the Treasury Robert A. Wallace, in charge of coinage, blamed speculators. He said that they were "buying up coins from the banks and the customers of banks by the roll and bag in anticipation of their potential increase in value on account of the coin shortage." A *New York Times* report of July 18, 1965, told of several coin dealers in the metropolitan area who were engaged in melting down coins for their silver content. Some speculators formed businesses interconnected by Teletype lines to communicate the latest price quotations of silver, thus stimulating the purchase and sale of coins for profit.

ATTEMPTS TO DEAL WITH THE SILVER SHORTAGE

The Treasury's considerable hoard of silver, about 1.7 billion ounces in mid-1964, helped to prevent speculators from making the profits they had hoped for. The huge silver reserve enabled the Treasury to sell silver on the open market to commercial users at the set ceiling price of $1.29 an ounce. This price had been set by the Treasury on September 9, 1963, as one of the steps to prevent the price of silver from rising. (The price had previously been set at the much lower level of 91 cents an ounce.) The main goal was to hold the price by free sales to keep it from rising above $1.38 an ounce. At that point the value of silver in U.S. coins would be equal to their face value.

However, despite all efforts to hold down the price of silver so that enough silver coins could be kept in circulation, silver stocks continued to dwindle. The Treasury holdings, which had in 1964 amounted to 1.7 billion ounces, were down to 1.19 billion ounces in January 1965. At that time an authority on coinage, Dr. V. Clain-Stefanelli, of the U.S. National Museum in Washington, pointed out that the free world in 1963 consumed 170 million more ounces of silver than it produced in the mines. He added that "the prospect of a long-term improvement of the silver supply situation is slim."

"Clad" or "sandwich" coins were authorized by the Coinage Act of July 1965 as a means of eliminating or reducing the amount of silver in U.S. coins. These coins were created by bonding a layer of one metal to each side of a central core of a second metal which was less valuable. By this act, silver was completely eliminated in the dimes and quarters, which up to 1965 had been composed of 90 per cent pure silver. It was specified that the new 10- and 25-cent pieces should be composed of an outer layer of copper and nickel (75 per cent copper and 25 per cent nickel), bonded to an inner core of pure copper. The half dollar, which had also contained 90 per cent pure silver, at the same time became a clad coin of only 40 per cent pure silver. It had an outer layer of a mixture of 80 per cent silver and 20 per cent copper, and an inner core of 79 per cent copper and 21 per cent silver. Thus, it would be the only new coin to continue the silver tradition, even in a modest way.

It was difficult for the nation to face having its silver coins lose all or most of the metal that had been a mainstay in its coinage system since its establishment in 1792. However, a number of other countries had set a precedent for clad coins. Canada had made steel "nickels" with chrome plating during the last two years of World War II in order to conserve nickel. West Germany, in 1948, had made 1-, 5-, and 10-pfennig pieces of steel planchets coated with copper alloy.

The U.S. Treasury and the mint had made considerable preparations in anticipation that new coins would be authorized. They nevertheless faced the titanic job of getting the new mint machinery in working order. Soon, however, the new dimes and quarters, the most useful of the coins, were pouring from the mints at Philadelphia, Denver, and San Francisco. (The San Francisco Mint, which had discontinued coinage in 1955, had been reactivated in the emergency.) The mints were working on a seven-day-week, twenty-four-hour-day schedule, which had been established in 1964 when the "crash" coinage program began. In October 1966, the mints established a monthly record by producing 1,094,326 coins of all denominations.

FURTHER GOVERNMENTAL STEPS
Unprecedented silver purchases, which threatened complete exhaustion of the reserves, caused the

Treasury to gradually restrict its sale. On May 18, 1967, the Treasury announced that it would sell silver only to domestic concerns using it in their businesses. It then also invoked its legal authority to prohibit "melting, treatment, and export of silver coins" under the penalty of a fine of "not more than $10,000, or imprisonment of not more than five years."

At that time the Treasury expressed the view that "widespread hoarding of silver coins had been prevented, in the main, by selling silver out of the Treasury's stocks to all purchasers—foreign and domestic—at $1.29 an ounce." But, having only 54.5 million ounces of "free silver" left on May 17, the Treasury had been forced to restrict the sales. The remainder of the reserves of the metal, of course, was tied up as backing for the $553 million silver certificates then outstanding. In June 1967, Congress passed a law calling for the complete redemption and retirement by June 24, 1968, of this paper money, which had been in process of redemption for several years. It also added 150 million dollars' worth of silver to the Treasury's reserves by "writing off" that amount of silver certificates deemed "lost or destroyed" through the years.

Could the U.S. Mint make enough of the new clad coins to overcome the continuing loss of old silver coins it might suffer? Could it at the same time free itself from the burden of keeping the price of silver at $1.29 an ounce, which had helped to keep the old silver coins in circulation? The dramatic answer to these questions came in a Treasury announcement on July 14, 1967: "Success of the Treasury Department's coinage program in producing silverless 'clad' coins in numbers which can meet any foreseeable needs has led to the decision to halt Treasury sales of silver at $1.29 an ounce."

The statement added that "future sales of silver will be at the going market price in amounts up to 2 million ounces a week." The order, subject to change, made silver available in limited amounts to small as well as large prospective purchasers on a competitive basis by means of "sealed bids." It would thus continue to help hold down the market price. Persons holding silver certificates, however, were still allowed to exchange them for silver at the $1.29 rate.

The lid was off the price of silver. Almost immediately it skyrocketed to $1.80 an ounce and above, then slumped below that level and later wavered in uncertain fashion. Speculators began buying up silver paper money at attractive prices in the hope of handsome profits. Cashiers and money-changers in banks and retail establishments tried to spot the vanishing bills, as did many other profit-minded individuals. These were exciting days for collectors!

SUCCESS OF THE TREASURY'S PROGRAM

The new coinage program had apparently been eminently successful. In July 1967 it was estimated by the Treasury that 70 per cent of its production goal for new clad coins had been achieved. In less than two years after the mints had begun turning out the new money, 8,250,000,000 silverless dimes and quarters had been struck, compared with 12,500,000,000 minted over the previous twenty-five years. The Treasury also predicted that the production of these pieces would top the 10 billion mark before the end of 1967, with 300 million coins minted monthly. This amount could be increased to 700 million monthly, if necessary.

The emergency having been largely met, the mints reduced their workweek to a five-day week of normal hours. It was believed that production of 6 billion coins in 1968 would suffice to keep the nation's economy rolling, even though the billions of old silver coins still in circulation might disappear sooner or later. Nevertheless, the government did not want all of the old high-silver content coins to get into the hands of speculators. The Treasury, through the Federal Reserve banks, began quietly withdrawing many of these coins from circulation, explaining that, if they were needed during the Christmas shopping rush or another emergency they could be put back into circulation.

The Treasury had been unable to prevent the crippling disappearance of silver coins in 1852 and 1862. In the mid-1960's it solved the problem in time to avoid what otherwise might have been a national calamity.

It is not easy to predict what will happen to the remaining U.S. coins of high silver content. Even the half dollar, containing only 40 per cent pure silver, is being hoarded by the public. It seems reasonable, though, in view of trends in hoarding, that most, if not all, the old silver coins will disappear from circulation sooner or later. Many millions of those outstanding will eventually find their way back to the Federal Reserve banks and the Treasury, to be kept as a reserve or to be melted down for recoinage. If the government's ban on melting down coins should be lifted it would be easier for many hoarders and speculators to reap profits. It is to be hoped that this ban will not soon, if ever, be removed.

The mint has indicated that the new half dollars of 40 per cent silver will continue to be made, and that more of them will enter circulation. However, since silverless quarters and dimes have proven highly acceptable, it may be only a matter of time before silverless halves will also be struck. Some members of Congress are strongly in favor of taking such a step to increase the Treasury's silver reserves. Certainly silver for future industrial and artistic uses, as well as national defense, is needed, and the supply of the metal is increasingly limited.

SUMMARY

In the twentieth century the American outlook toward money has become more complex and sophisticated to match the growth of American culture. Much more attention has been paid to making sure U.S. money meets acceptable international standards, because of the nation's increased overseas trade and growing involvement in world politics. In place of the relatively rigid standards of either gold or silver, a more flexible system of managed money has come into being. Much of the monetary upheaval that formerly took place in the business world is now forestalled quietly behind the scenes by the Federal Reserve System. In this way many of the financial disasters that were previously beyond control can now be avoided. The ability and willingness to make good our money—that is, our credit—has become much more important than possession of a specific amount of gold or silver for each piece of paper. The dollar has become an international currency recognized and desired by friend and foe alike. Truly, in the last fifty years America's money has come of age.

# APPENDIX

# THE HOBBY OF
# COIN COLLECTING

Though this book is intended primarily for those interested in studying the history of the United States as reflected in its coinage, it also has the purpose of providing helpful information for the collector of coins and money, for the really serious collector—the numismatist—is eager to know the origin and background of the items he collects. Often the collector begins in the hope of making a profit, intrigued with the idea that his coins will increase in value. He may never rise above the level of an accumulator, monotonously poring over coin price lists. However, if he will study the pieces he acquires and learn more about their history, he will increase his knowledge through his collection. Pursued in this way, coin collecting becomes not only a profitable hobby but a fascinating, educational pastime.

To understand the origin, legends, and designs of a piece of money is to make it come alive in terms of people and events. It becomes far more than a piece of metal with a particular monetary value. Indeed, a numismatic collection supplies both the means and the motive for enjoyable study of aspects of history, art, economics, politics, and finance. Individual coins can lead an inquisitive collector to an interest in an endless variety of subjects, from mythology to architecture, from archaeology to heraldry.

COLLECTORS AND THEIR ORGANIZATIONS

It has been estimated that from five million to seven million people in the United States collect coins for one reason or another. Though only a small number may be truly classified as numismatists, coin collectors range from teen-agers to senior citizens and include people from every walk of life. Although coin collecting has steadily grown in this country for more than a century, it has truly become one of the nation's most popular pastimes only in recent years. Studies indicate that there are possibly four to five times as many who collect coins today as in the late 1950's, when the collecting "fever" seems to have started in a big way. The wave of speculation in silver, which began at about that time (see Chapter 15), no doubt helped to spur the enthusiasm for collecting, creating new highs in demand for all kinds of U.S. coins and those of other nations, too. This increased interest, quite naturally, drove up the prices paid for coins, which reached a peak in 1964 and 1965. Later, many coins were found to be overpriced and a period of readjustment followed.

Lower prices were established for the more common coin classifications and the collectors became more selective, seeking only the rarer and more desirable items.

Serious collectors have banded together in coin clubs and other numismatic organizations. The growth of these groups in recent years is an indication of the ever-increasing popularity of coin collecting. Largest of all numismatic groups in the country is the American Numismatic Association, founded in 1891. At the end of June 1967, the A.N.A. had more than twenty-four thousand members, both individuals and coin clubs, from every state of the Union and seven foreign countries. But only a small percentage of the millions of coin collectors belong to the fifteen hundred coin clubs and other numismatic groups in the U.S., or subscribe to the publications printed for those who collect coins and other forms of money. Many of the more prominent collectors belong to the American Numismatic Society, founded in 1858, oldest and most respected of the numismatic groups. At its headquarters in New York City, the A.N.S. has one of the largest numismatic libraries in the world and one of the world's greatest collections of coins. Both the A.N.A. and the A.N.S. have been instrumental in bringing numismatics in this country to its present high level.

It is likely that people have collected coins since ancient times. It is known that coin collecting started in a serious way during the Italian Renaissance and

spread throughout Europe in the fifteenth and six-
teenth centuries. As might be expected, the hobby
was for a long time confined to persons of noble
birth, or at least of education, wealth, and power.

PUBLICATIONS FOR COLLECTORS

Numismatics had relatively late beginnings in the
United States. American collectors did not become
numerous until the 1850's, although there were a
few enthusiasts who collected earlier. At about this
time there appeared several important books on
coins: John H. Hickcox's *History of American Coinage* (1858) , Charles Ira Bushnell's monograph on
early merchants' tokens, and Montroville Wilson
Dickeson's *American Numismatic Manual,* which
was printed in 1859, 1860, and 1865 and had considerable popularity. The American Numismatic
Society was a key factor in early research efforts.
Such scholars as Sylvester Crosby, who concentrated
on the study of colonial coins and in 1875 published
*Early Coins of America,* produced books which even
today are regarded as classics for the numismatic
student.

Officials of the U.S. Mint were quite aware of the
importance of collecting coins. Adam Eckfeldt, chief
coiner at the mint from 1814 to 1838, began the
Mint Cabinet Collection in 1838, donating to it odd,
rare, and choice pieces that he had been saving since
1792. James Ross Snowden, director of the mint
from 1853 to 1861, published *Mint Manual* and

*Washington and National Medals,* both quite popular with collectors.

Today there are literally hundreds of coin books, published studies in numismatics, and price lists of coin dealers (estimated in 1964 by *Pace Numismatic Financial Weekly* to number about eleven thousand). Yeoman's *A Guide Book of United States Coins,* known among collectors as "the Red Book," is undoubtedly the most popular annual volume. It lists average coin prices based upon a survey of those listed by many dealers, as well as other valuable information. Major publications on coins include the weekly *Coin World,* which was founded in 1960 and at one time had as many as 128 pages and a circulation of 160,000. Among important coin magazines are *The Numismatist,* published by the A.N.A., *Numismatic Scrapbook Magazine,* and *COINage,* the last-named having about 180,000 circulation.

Growth of the hobby of coin collecting as a form of investment has resulted in the widespread use of Teletype networks to link the larger coin dealers, thus providing up-to-the-minute quotations on the prices and availability of certain coins as well as the transmission and confirmation of orders between dealers. Coin shows and conventions where collectors and dealers meet have also mushroomed over the country in recent years. These gatherings feature educational activities, including numismatic exhibits and talks by authorities.

COINS FOR COLLECTORS

The condition of a coin, as well as its rarity, is a primary factor in determining its value. The collector wants the finest coins for his display. A brilliant uncirculated coin, therefore, is worth far more than a piece in poor condition. A *proof* coin, which has a mirrorlike surface (struck with polished dies on polished blanks), made by the U.S. Mint primarily for collectors and in limited quantities, is usually worth more than an ordinary brand-new piece intended for general circulation.

The U.S. Mint began making proof coins in 1858 and, with some interruptions, has continued production of these attractive pieces. Because they cost more to produce than the coins intended for circulation, the proofs, quite naturally, have been sold by the mint at a premium. A package set of the current coins for any year was often priced at twice face value plus mailing costs. In the past the proof coins were made only at the Philadelphia Mint. Because of the ever increasing demand for such coins, however, this function has been taken over by the San Francisco Mint, which is better equipped to perform the task.

Proof sets were struck by the mint continuously from 1858 to 1916. Production was resumed in 1936, but discontinued in 1942 because of the wartime coin shortage and the necessity of using all the mint machinery for making regular coins and service medals. The manufacture of proofs was resumed in 1950, but production was again halted during the recent coin shortage in 1964, and resumed only in 1968. During the three-year interval, however, attractive nonproof "special mint sets" were issued by the mint for collectors.

Because of their limited quantity, proofs have generally been considered as a "good buy" by the collector, hence the markedly increased demand for them in recent years, which in turn has led to increased production. In 1936 only 3,837 proof sets were struck. This number was about tripled in 1940; it grew to 51,386 in 1950; then in 1960 it climbed to 1,691,000 sets, and continued above the 3 million level until it reached nearly 4 million sets in 1964. Thus proof coins, fairly rare items in 1936, have become numerous in the 1960's.

For many years, until 1964, "mint sets" were also made available by the mint in limited quantities for collectors. These were nothing more than sets made up from coins intended for regular circulation.

### COMMEMORATIVE COINS

Commemorative coins, as their name indicates, were issued to mark special occasions and to honor great men and outstanding historic events. Many countries have issued them during the past century and some were issued during earlier periods. American commemoratives are numerous and include some of the handsomest and most unusual of all U.S. coins.

The United States issued its first commemorative coin in 1892, the half dollar marking the World's Columbian Exposition in Chicago and the 400th anniversary of the discovery of America by Christopher Columbus. In 1954 the last of the series of half dollars commemorating the lives of Booker T. Washington and George Washington Carver was struck. In the 62 years between those dates the U.S. Mint produced a total of 157 commemorative coins of 60 major types in silver and gold. These include 1 quarter, 142 half dollars (48 types), 1 silver dollar, 9 gold dollars (6 types), 2 quarter eagles ($2.50), and 2 $50 gold pieces.

The commemoratives, like the proofs, are produced in restricted quantities and seldom seen in circulation. However, unlike the proofs, which were struck for collectors only, the commemorative pieces have a wide interest. Cherished by nearly all collectors, they are also held as keepsakes by thousands of historically minded individuals with a special interest in the events or persons being memorialized. Like the proofs, commemoratives were sold to the public at prices above their face value, generally at twice face value or more. Instead of being distributed by the mint, however, they have generally been sold through the agencies in charge of the respective commemorations as a means of raising funds to finance activities connected with the commemoration.

Congress must give its approval before a commemorative coin can be struck at the mint. The commemorative is coined at face value for the group handling its sale. Many of the most important events in American history are recalled through these coins, though in some cases the events and persons memorialized are of only local importance. There have sometimes been abuses in the practice, especially where issuance has been prolonged over a number of years, producing coins bearing different dates and mintmarks. Such a practice has no purpose other than profit for the promoters at the expense and frustration of the collector. The original significance of the date of commemoration is lost by continued reissuance of the coins. The awareness of such abuses has led to the present policy of the United States not to issue commemorative coins and to recommend future reliance upon the use of medals to commemorate historic events. A statement by the Treasury Department in 1964 defined its position: "The Treasury Department has consistently opposed the enactment of legislation authorizing the minting of commemorative coins. It is the position of the Department that these issues conflict with the purpose for which the coinage system was established, namely, to provide a medium of exchange; and that they lead to indefensible abuses, notably traffic in them for private gain."

After the enactment of legislation prohibiting the issuance of commemorative coins authorized prior to March 1, 1939, Congress did relent in 1946 and authorized the Iowa Statehood Centennial and the

Booker T. Washington commemorative half dollars. The latter coin, the first U.S. coin to bear the likeness of a Negro (also the first designed by a Negro —Isaac Scott Hathaway), was issued in various quantities at the different mints until 1951. It was redesigned as the Washington-Carver half dollar and reissued under the same authority. The last of the pieces was struck in 1954. Since then no other U.S. commemorative coin has been issued.

Meanwhile medals, which have been used for hundreds of years in marking historic events and honoring famous people, have taken the place of coins in American commemorations. Through the years nearly all serious numismatists have collected medals as well as coins. For medals have a distinct advantage over coins in reproducing sculptured works of art in that they are unhampered by certain restrictions required in producing a coin. Medals are made by the U.S. Mint as well as by private concerns. The mint requires the approval of Congress before it can strike a medal, whereas private medal makers have no such restriction.

Whether medals will permanently replace coins for important future commemorations is difficult to foretell. There are many persons, including members of Congress as well as collectors, who frequently clamor for a return to commemorative coins. The following list of U.S. commemorative coins briefly indicates the nature of the events memorialized and the people honored during the sixty-two years when such coins were struck. Since many of the coins originally struck were later melted down because of a lack of demand for them, only the net coinage figures, representing those now in the hands of collectors or held by others as keepsakes, are given.

---

## U.S. COMMEMORATIVE COINS
### (1892–1954)

| | When Issued | Net Coinage * |
|---|---|---|
| *Silver* <br> *Quarter Dollar* | | |
| Isabella Quarter Dollar (Columbian Exposition) | 1893 | 24,214 |
| *Silver* <br> *Half Dollars* | | |
| Columbian Exposition | 1892 | 950,000 |
| | 1893 | 1,550,405 |
| Panama-Pacific Exposition | 1915 S mint | 27,134 |
| Lincoln-Illinois Centennial | 1918 | 100,058 |

* Does not include coins minted but later melted.

| | | |
|---|---|---:|
| Maine Centennial | 1920 | 50,028 |
| Pilgrim | | |
| Tercentenary | 1920 | 152,112 |
| | 1921 | 20,053 |
| Missouri | | |
| Centennial | 1921 (2★4 type) | 5,000 |
| | (without 2★4) | 15,428 |
| Alabama | | |
| Centennial | 1921 (2x2 type) | 6,606 |
| | (without 2x2) | 59,038 |
| Grant Memorial | 1922 (with star) | 4,256 |
| | (without star) | 67,405 |
| Monroe Doctrine | | |
| Centennial | 1923 S mint | 274,077 |
| Huguenot- | | |
| Walloon | | |
| Tercentenary | 1924 | 142,080 |
| Lexington- | | |
| Concord | | |
| Sesquicen- | | |
| tennial | 1925 | 162,013 |
| Stone Mountain | 1925 | 1,314,709 |
| California Dia- | | |
| mond Jubilee | 1924 S mint | 86,594 |
| Fort Vancouver | | |
| Centennial | 1925 | 14,994 |
| Sesquicentennial | | |
| of American | | |
| Independence | 1926 | 141,120 |

| | | |
|---|---|---:|
| Oregon Trail Memorial | 1926 | 47,955 |
| | 1926 S mint | 83,055 |
| (All coins of | 1928 | 6,028 |
| same general | 1933 D mint | 5,008 |
| type) | 1934 D mint | 7,006 |
| | 1936 | 10,006 |
| | 1936 S mint | 5,006 |
| | 1937 D mint | 12,008 |
| | 1938 | 6,006 |
| | 1938 D mint | 6,005 |
| | 1938 S mint | 6,006 |
| | 1939 | 3,004 |
| | 1939 D mint | 3,004 |
| | 1939 S mint | 3,005 |
| Vermont Sesquicenten-nial (Battle of Bennington) | 1927 | 28,142 |
| Hawaii Sesquicenten-nial | 1928 | 10,008 |
| | 1928 (proof pieces) | 50 |
| Maryland Tercentenary | 1934 | 25,015 |
| Texas Indepen-dence Centen-nial | 1934 | 61,350 |
| | 1935 | 9,994 |
| (All coins of same general type) | 1935 D mint | 10,007 |
| | 1935 S mint | 10,008 |

|  | 1936 | 8,911 |
|---|---|---|
|  | 1936 D mint | 9,039 |
|  | 1936 S mint | 9,064 |
|  | 1937 | 6,571 |
|  | 1937 D mint | 6,605 |
|  | 1937 S mint | 6,637 |
|  | 1938 | 3,780 |
|  | 1938 D mint | 3,775 |
|  | 1938 S mint | 3,816 |

| Daniel Boone Bicentennial | 1934 | 10,007 |
|---|---|---|
|  | 1935 | 10,010 |
| (All coins of | 1935 D mint | 5,005 |
| same general | 1935 S mint | 5,005 |
| type) | 1935 † | 10,008 |
|  | 1935 D mint † | 2,003 |
|  | 1935 S mint † | 2,004 |
|  | 1936 | 12,012 |
|  | 1936 D mint | 5,005 |
|  | 1936 S mint | 5,006 |
|  | 1937 | 9,810 |
|  | 1937 D mint | 2,506 |
|  | 1937 S mint | 2,506 |
|  | 1938 | 2,100 |
|  | 1938 D mint | 2,100 |
|  | 1938 S mint | 2,100 |

| Connecticut Tercentenary | 1935 | 25,018 |
|---|---|---|

† Small 1934 on reverse.

| | | |
|---|---|---:|
| Arkansas | | |
|     Centennial | 1935 | 13,012 |
| | 1935 D mint | 5,505 |
| (All coins of | 1935 S mint | 5,506 |
| same general | 1936 ‡ | 9,660 |
| type) | 1936 D mint ‡ | 9,660 |
| | 1936 S mint ‡ | 9,662 |
| | 1937 | 5,505 |
| | 1937 D  mint | 5,505 |
| | 1937 S mint | 5,506 |
| | 1938 | 3,156 |
| | 1938 D mint | 3,155 |
| | 1938 S mint | 3,156 |
| | 1939 | 2,104 |
| | 1939 D mint | 2,104 |
| | 1939 S mint | 2,105 |
| Robinson-Arkan- | | |
|     sas Centennial | 1936 | 25,265 |
| Hudson, New | | |
|     York, Sesqui- | | |
|     centennial | 1935 | 10,008 |
| California-Pacific | | |
|     International | | |
|     Exposition | | |
|     (San Diego) | 1935 S mint | 70,132 |
| | 1936 D mint | 30,092 |
| Old Spanish | | |
|     Trail (400th | | |
|     anniversary) | 1935 | 10,008 |

‡ 1936 on reverse.

| | | |
|---|---|---|
| Rhode Island Tercentenary (Providence) | 1936 | 20,013 |
| | 1936 D mint | 15,010 |
| | 1936 S mint | 15,011 |
| Cleveland Great Lakes Exposition | 1936 | 50,030 |
| Wisconsin Territorial Centennial | 1936 | 25,015 |
| Cincinnati Musical Center | 1936 | 5,005 |
| | 1936 D mint | 5,005 |
| | 1936 S mint | 5,006 |
| Long Island Tercentenary | 1936 | 81,826 |
| Bridgeport, Connecticut, Centennial | 1936 | 25,015 |
| York County, Maine, Tercentenary | 1936 | 25,015 |
| Lynchburg, Virginia, Sesquicentennial | 1936 | 20,013 |
| Elgin, Illinois, Centennial | 1936 | 20,015 |

| | | |
|---|---|---|
| Albany, New York, Charter (250th anniversary) | 1936 | 17,671 |
| San Francisco-Oakland Bay Bridge | 1936 S mint | 71,424 |
| Columbia, South Carolina, Sesquicentennial | 1936 | 9,007 |
| | 1936 D mint | 8,009 |
| | 1936 S mint | 8,007 |
| Delaware Tercentenary | 1936 | 20,993 |
| Battle of Gettysburg | 1936 | 26,928 |
| Norfolk, Virginia, Bicentennial | 1937 (dated 1936) | 16,936 |
| Roanoke Island, North Carolina (350th anniversary) | 1937 | 29,030 |
| Battle of Antietam (75th anniversary) | 1937 | 18,028 |
| New Rochelle, New York (250th anniversary) | 1938 | 15,266 |
| Iowa Statehood Centennial | 1946 | 100,057 |

| | | |
|---|---|---|
| Booker T. Washington Memorial | 1946 | 1,000,546 § |
| | 1946 D mint | 200,113 |
| (All coins of | 1946 S mint | 500,279 |
| same general | 1947 ‖ | 100,017 |
| type) | 1947 D mint ‖ | 100,017 |
| | 1947 S mint ‖ | 100,017 |
| | 1948 | 8,005 |
| | 1948 D mint ‖ | 8,005 |
| | 1948 S mint ‖ | 8,005 |
| | 1949 ‖ | 6,004 |
| | 1949 D mint ‖ | 6,004 |
| | 1949 S mint ‖ | 6,004 |
| | 1950 ‖ | 6,004 |
| | 1950 D mint | 6,004 |
| | 1950 S mint | 512,091 |
| | 1951 ‖ | 510,082 |
| | 1951 D mint | 7,004 |
| | 1951 S mint | 7,004 |
| Washington-Carver ¶ | 1951 | 110,018 |
| | 1951 D mint | 10,004 |
| (All coins of | 1951 S mint | 10,004 |
| same general | 1952 | 2,006,292 |
| type) | 1952 D mint | 8,006 |
| | 1952 S mint | 8,006 |

§ This is a gross figure; number melted is unknown.
‖ 1946 type.
¶ Commemorating the lives of Booker T. Washington and George Washington Carver.

|  | 1953 | 8,003 |
|---|---|---|
|  | 1953 D mint | 8,003 |
|  | 1953 S mint | 108,020 |
|  | 1954 | 12,006 |
|  | 1954 D mint | 12,006 |
|  | 1954 S mint | 122,024 |

*Silver Dollar*

| Lafayette Dollar | 1900 | 36,026 |
|---|---|---|

*Gold Dollars*

| Louisiana Purchase (reverse same for both coins) | 1903 (Jefferson face) | 17,500 |
|---|---|---|
|  | 1903  (McKinley face) | 17,500 |
| Lewis and Clark Centennial Exposition | 1904 | 10,025 |
|  | 1905 | 10,041 |
| Panama-Pacific Exposition | 1915 S mint | 15,000 |
| McKinley Memorial | 1916 | 9,977 |
|  | 1917 | 10,000 |
| Grant Memorial | 1922 (with star) | 5,016 |
|  | 1922 (without star) | 5,000 |

*Gold*
*Quarter Eagles*

| | | |
|---|---|---|
| Panama-Pacific Exposition | 1915 S mint | 6,749 |
| Philadelphia Sesquicentennial | 1926 | 46,019 |

*Gold*
*Fifty Dollars*

| | | |
|---|---|---|
| Panama-Pacific Exposition | 1915 S mint (round) | 483 |
| | 1915 S mint (octagonal) | 645 |

# GLOSSARY

BARTER. Trading one set of goods or services for another. (Compare this term with *commodity money*.)

BEADING. A rounded rim projecting slightly from the surface of a coin. Beading is usually a decorative device and does not have a practical purpose, as does *milling*.

BIMETALLISM. The policy of using two metals (usually gold and silver) at one time as a standard for currency. The ratio of values between these two metals is fixed by law. Their respective market values may change, however, so the ratio hardly ever remains accurate.

CIRCULATION. The free movement of money from person to person in buying and selling, payment of debts, and other common uses.

CLAD COIN. A coin in which two outer layers of a precious metal, such as silver, are bonded to a central core of less valuable metal. Another name for a clad coin is "sandwich coin."

CLIPPING. The practice of scraping away some of the metal from around the edge of a coin where the loss is difficult to detect, especially if the edge is smooth. See *milling*.

COMMODITY MONEY. A currency substitute that consists of some commonly acceptable article, such as corn or tobacco, and is used in payment for other goods or services. (Compare this term with *barter*.)

CURRENCY. Any coin, paper note, or other object whose primary purpose is to serve as a medium of exchange. Sometimes a common article, such as tobacco or nails, will be called currency when used as a medium of exchange, but it is more correctly termed commodity money.

DEBASE. To reduce the intrinsic value of a coin by reducing the amount of precious metal contained in it. For instance, if the amount of silver in a half dollar is reduced from fifty cents' worth to thirty cents' worth, the coin is said to be debased.

DEPRECIATION. The decrease in value of a currency to an amount lower than that printed on its surface. Depreciation usually occurs when the price of the precious metal that backs a currency is reduced on the world market. (Compare this term with *devaluation*.)

DEVALUATION. The reduction of the amount of precious metal with which a government agrees to back a particular currency. (Compare this term with *depreciation*.)

DIE. A hollow form or block in which metal is encased to shape it into coins; also, the positive forms from which these hollow blocks are constructed.

FACE. The side of a coin generally thought of as the front. It derives its name from the almost universal custom of decorating this side with the bust (or face) of a historical or mythical personage. The face is often called the *obverse*. The opposite side is the *reverse*.

FACE VALUE. The worth of a piece as printed on its face. This figure represents the amount in precious metal or other lawful money for which it can be redeemed.

FINENESS. The percentage of pure precious metal used in the manufacture of a coin as opposed to any alloys which are added to give strength or hardness to the piece. A coin $11\frac{1}{12}$ fine contains 11 parts precious metal to one part alloy.

FRACTIONAL CURRENCY NOTE. Paper currency used during certain periods in the same manner as a fractional piece. Examples are *postage currency notes* and *shinplasters*.

FRACTIONAL PIECE. A coin which has a value less than that of the basic unit of a currency. In the United States, where the dollar is the basic denomination, fractional pieces are the half dollar, quarter, dime, nickel, and penny. See *subsidiary coin*.

GOLD CERTIFICATE. Originally, any note issued by the Secretary of the Treasury indicating that an equivalent amount of gold would be paid upon demand. Since 1934, gold certificates have been used solely within the Federal Reserve System.

GRAIN. One seven-thousandth of a pound. This measure was originally derived from the weight of a grain of wheat.

GREENBACK. A legal-tender note of a kind first issued in 1862. Greenbacks were so called because the backs of the bills were printed in green ink.

HARD MONEY. A general designation for coins or metal money as opposed to paper. The term is also used to mean currency that is backed by an equivalent amount of gold (as opposed to less expensive silver) and is therefore very stable in value.

INFLATION. A situation wherein money depreciates, and more currency is needed to purchase a given amount of goods or services than has previously been necessary. Thus, the prices of commodities are said to become "inflated" in relation to the value of the currency in use.

INTRINSIC VALUE. Value of a coin as established by the amount of precious metal it contains. This value will vary with fluctuations in the market value of the precious metal, and has nothing to do with the *face value* of the coin.

LEGAL TENDER. Any form of currency designated by law as acceptable in the payment of debts.

MILLING. A series of tiny ridges and grooves around the edge of a coin. Milling defines the exact edge of a coin and makes it easy to detect the practice of *clipping*.

266

OBVERSE. See *face*.

PATTERN PIECE. A coin struck from an experimental die in order to determine whether it will be adopted as an official piece and manufactured in large quantities to be put into circulation.

POSTAGE CURRENCY NOTE. A short-lived form of paper money in denominations of less than one dollar issued during the Civil War to relieve a shortage of coins. These notes replaced the ordinary postage stamps that were used briefly in lieu of small change. Postage currency notes were so named because they carried reproductions of current stamp designs and even had perforated edges. They were superseded by *fractional currency notes*.

PRIVATE COINAGE. Coins manufactured by a private individual or company as opposed to those minted by a state or national government. See *token*.

REAL VALUE. The intrinsic value of a coin, based upon the current price of its precious metal content. Also, the amount any currency is worth at a given time in terms of its buying power.

REDEMPTION. The act of exchanging a piece of currency for its designated value in precious metal or lawful money.

REVERSE. The side of a coin usually thought of as the back. The opposite side is called the *face* or obverse.

SANDWICH COIN. See *clad coin*.

SCRIP. A paper certificate issued in place of payment in legal tender. Originally the term was used to designate a note promising to pay a debt. Gradually it came to be used for any paper certificate with a small face value. The term is most accurately applied to private paper note issues, but after the Civil War often was used for U.S. fractional currency notes as well. See *shinplaster*.

SEIGNIORAGE. The government's profit on the manufacture of coins. Seigniorage is the difference between the face value of a coin and the amount it costs a mint to manufacture it. The term is derived from the French word meaning "right of the lord" and is thought to refer to the monarch's custom of demanding a portion of precious metal for each coin struck.

SHINPLASTER. Any piece of *scrip*. The term refers especially to privately issued paper currency that is weakly backed or depreciated in value. The name indicates the public's lack of faith in such money.

SOFT MONEY. Currency that is inferior, insufficiently supported, or generally worth only a portion of its face value. See *hard money*.

SPECIE. The general name given to coinage as opposed to paper money. Also, all coins of a specific denomination.

STANDARD. The precious metal with which a government guarantees to back its currency.

STRIKE. To make coins out of metal. The term describes the process of punching the metal with a heavy die or pattern in order to make an impression in the form of the desired coin, which is thereby cut out of the metal.

SUBSIDIARY COIN. A coin that contains precious metal worth less than its *face value*. Such coins are usually of small denomination and have limited legal-tender value. That is, they are redeemable at stated worth only up to a certain sum. Subsidiary coins tend to stay in circulation for a long time because they cannot be profitably melted down by speculators and are not intrinsically valuable enough to be hoarded.

SWEATING. Heating a metal coin in order to extract, in liquid form, some of its gold or silver content. This is possible because the softer precious metal will melt at a lower temperature than the less valuable alloy with which it is mixed.

TOKEN. A type of coin, usually of little intrinsic value, that is issued either by a private company or a government in place of legal tender. The usefulness of tokens depends solely on the faith with which their users accept the maker's intention to redeem them at their stated worth. In colonial America many tokens were produced to relieve the shortage of legally backed coinage.

# INDEX

*Note:* Italic figures indicate illustration.

DATE DUE